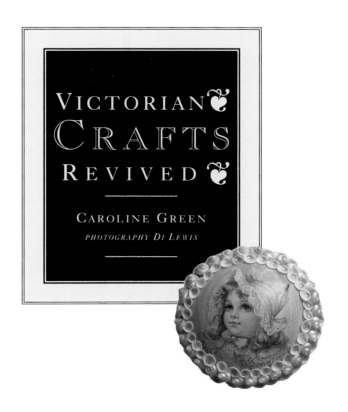

VICTORIAN CRAFTS REVIVED

CAROLINE GREEN

PHOTOGRAPHY DI LEWIS

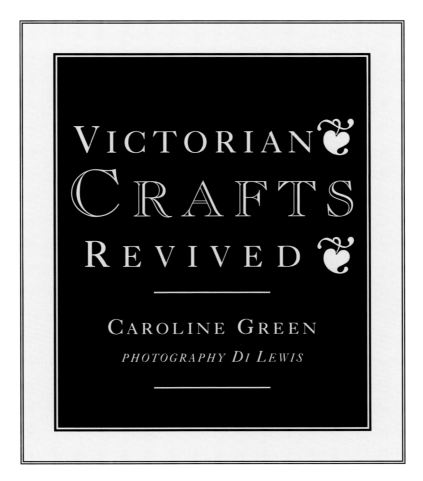

VICTORIAN CRAFTS REVIVED

CAROLINE GREEN

PHOTOGRAPHY DI LEWIS

David & Charles

A DAVID & CHARLES BOOK

First published in the UK in 1993
First published in paperback 2003
reprinted 2003

Text and designs Copyright © Caroline Green 1993,
2003 (unless otherwise credited - see
Acknowledgements)
Photography Copyright © David & Charles 1993, 2003

Distributed in North America
by F&W Publications, Inc.
4700 East Galbraith Road
Cincinnati, OH 45236
1-800-289-0963

A catalogue record for this book is available from the
British Library
ISBN 0 7153 1510 2

Typeset by Greenshires Icon Exeter
Printed in Singapore by KHL Printing Co Pte Ltd
for David & Charles
Brunel House Newton Abbot Devon

Contents

Foreword

I have always admired the Victorians for their love of intricate detailed pattern and rich colours.

The fascination started at the age of ten when my great aunt, who was born in Victoria's reign, gave me a miniature antique chest of drawers for my birthday. I was thrilled with it and immediately vowed to keep it full of tiny, precious items that I could collect over the years. I began with silver-topped scent bottles, miniature books, thimbles, snuff boxes and any tiny article that I could afford with my pocket money or beg from a generous grandfather. I still have the chest of drawers today; however, it only houses a small part of the collection that I started then.

As I grew older, I became interested in all types of sewing and crafts and so my collection included the beautiful tools and sewing items that were produced in such profusion in Victorian times.

My interest grew until needlework and crafts became my career and at last I have brought everything together to write this book that I hope will bring you many hours of creative pleasure.

Introduction

The industrial revolution brought a greater amount of leisure time to the newly rich middle-class women who could now afford to employ servants. So needlework and crafts were no longer just for the gentry. The newly established middle-class lady of the household had time on her hands to produce beautiful pieces of needlework, watercolours, cut paperwork, embroidery, shellwork and flowercrafts. The daughters of the house, with little chance of a career before marriage, also learned these skills. The items they made so beautifully were displayed about the home to be admired by family and friends. They were a source of great pride to both the maker and her husband or father.

In the middle of the nineteenth century extravagantly coloured, printed charts for woolwork arrived from Germany. This was quite a revolution to home needlework for up until that time ladies had spent long hours making delicate embroidered silk pictures in crewel work. Sometimes the silk pictures were pre-drawn, ready to be translated into stitching, but more often they were designed at home. Some people looked down on the new, ready-made patterns from the continent as lacking in creativity and artistic talent, but in fact they brought needlework to a much wider audience.

New chemical, aniline dyes meant that the wool colours could be much brighter than the vegetable dyes used in the past and the Victorians made full use of every shade! The results must have been very vivid and not the subtle, faded colours that we now associate with Victorian furnishings.

Almost every sort of household item could be made in needlepoint and it soon became the most popular of all pastimes. Large drawing room carpets were probably the most ambitious projects although they were mostly stitched in small squares and then assembled later into the full sized carpet. Cushions and covers for chairs and sofas were the most usual sight in a Victorian drawing room with the addition of bell-pulls, fire-screens, footstools, pictures and pelmets. Small beginners' projects ranged from pincushions, needlecases and book covers to waistcoats, slippers and cigar cases. Virtually the whole household's needs could be catered for in needlepoint!

Flowers were a popular subject, arranged into garlands, posies and wreaths. There are many original examples still surviving today. Exotic birds and animals were an excellent subject, as well as rather sentimental representations of pet dogs and cats which were a great favourite. Highly detailed copies of famous paintings and religious scenes were often stitched, especially on a Sunday when frivolous pastimes were frowned on.

All sorts of other needlework abounded, with cross stitch a great favourite and often the first type of stitching that a child learned. This was usually in the form of a sampler to perfect the stitch and try out various patterns.

Whitework embroidery was more a necessity

than a craft as it was the fashion for most table and bed-linen to be embroidered in this way for everyday use. All types of patchwork and quilting were very common. This filtered down into the lower classes too, where poorer women could make warm patchwork quilts from scraps of fabric cut from old clothes, thus making something beautiful from virtually nothing.

More frivolous crafts and fancy work, as it was known, were featured in the many ladies' magazines that were produced in that era. Ladies were encouraged to make all manner of workbaskets, pincushions, antimacassars, needlecases, even penwipers, whatnots and decorated matchboxes to fill their time. These were produced to give as Christmas and birthday presents and to sell in aid of various charities at bazaars. So perhaps things have not changed much in a century after all!

VICTORIAN SEWING EQUIPMENT

A lady's sewing table was given pride of place in the drawing room and many of them were exquisite pieces of furniture. However, if a sewing table was too expensive, a work-box could hold almost as much equipment and the number of different styles still in existence show that this was probably the most popular choice.

Beautiful sets of sewing accessories were made to go with these boxes and if you come across one today, with the set complete, it is a real find. Most sets were made of silver, mother-of-pearl or ivory and always included scissors, a thimble, a slim case of needles, a stiletto and a bodkin. These five essential items can often be found in small, flat recessed ivory boxes that could be slipped into a pocket for travelling. Ladies often took their sewing with them when visiting friends, especially if they didn't enjoy playing bridge or other games.

In addition to the basic sewing tools, thread winders, spools, hemming clamps, pincushions, pin boxes and tape measures were all thought to be necessary items for the needlewoman. Each of the items came in numerous different styles and ingenious designs and they make delightful collectors' pieces.

Patchwork & Quilting

Crib Quilt

Patchwork and quilting are two closely allied crafts that are typical of the Victorians' love of flamboyantly coloured and detailed work. Many patchwork items involve some sort of quilting to complete them but you can also make beautiful, highly decorative items by simply quilting plain fabric in intricate patterns.

This Baby block or Tumbling block patchwork was a great favourite on both sides of the Atlantic. It is worked in fine lawn, tacked on to diamond-shaped papers, then hand stitched in groups of three, to make the three dimensional-looking block pattern. The secret is to choose the fabrics very carefully in distinct groups of light, medium and dark colours. This design uses about twelve different patterns.

For a 59 × 40cm (23 × 15 ¾in) quilt, plus frill:
20cm (8in) each of fine patterned lawn in twelve
  different designs: 4 light, 4 medium and 4 dark
1m (1yd) of similar weight fabric for the frills and
  backing material
50cm (½yd) of thick polyester wadding
Cartridge paper for patchwork papers
Craft knife and metal ruler
Thick card for template
Sharp pencil
Matching threads
A paper pattern of your cot shape
Quilting needle and quilting thread to match fabrics
2 skeins of embroidery thread in toning colour

❶ Trace off the diamond shape from the page and use this to cut an accurate template in thick card. Draw round the template with a sharp pencil on to the cartridge paper. Then cut out about 110 paper diamonds to use as patchwork papers. Using the same template cut out the same number of diamonds in fabric adding about 6mm (¼in) all round for turning. The fabric does not have to be accurate as long as

there is enough to fold round the papers with a small seam allowance.

❷ Pin one paper diamond centrally on to the wrong side of each fabric diamond. Fold the excess fabric over the edge of the paper and tack (baste) it in position. Start the tacking (basting) with a knot on the right side of the diamond, as this will make it easier to remove the threads later on. Prepare a quantity of these pieces before you start to join them into the patchwork.

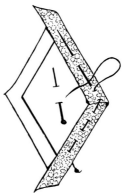

Stitching fabric to paper diamond

❸ Begin joining the pieces together in blocks of three, one light, one medium and one dark together in each group. Always have the light one at the top, the medium one to the left and

The quilt is decoratively edged with a matching frill and ruffle.

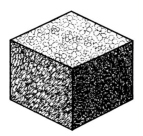

Block of diamond patches

the dark one on the right. To join two patches, place them with right sides facing and oversew with tiny stitches along one edge. At the end of the side, open the patches out flat and join on the other patch to form the hexagonal block. When you have made a quantity of these, lay them out to the size of your quilt pattern in a pleasing arrangement of colours. Join the blocks in horizontal rows and then join the rows together to make the complete shape.

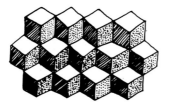

Join the blocks to make the traditional pattern

❹ When all the patches are sewn together, pull out the tacking (basting) threads by the knots and remove the patchwork papers. Carefully iron the resulting patchwork fabric. Cut out a piece of backing fabric and wadding to the same size as the quilt and tack them all together with

right sides outside and the wadding in between. Work several rows of tacking (basting) through all the layers, starting from the centre and working out to the edges.

❺ Using matching quilting thread and a quilting needle, make small running stitches in lines following the top and base of each row of blocks. This will join the layers together securely and quilt the patchwork. Pin all round the edge and cut out the quilting to the exact size of your cot pattern.

❻ For the frill, cut and join strips of the backing fabric, to make a piece 10cm × 4.50m (4in × 5yd). Fold this strip in half, with wrong sides together and run a gathering thread near the raw edges. Pull up the gathers to fit round the edge of the quilt and pin and stitch the frill to the back of the quilt, matching raw edges. Press the seam allowance towards the centre of the quilt to make the frill lie flat and then tack (paste) the raw edges down.

❼ For the ruffle, use one of the patchwork fabrics to cut and join strips, to make a piece 7.5cm × 4.50m (3in × 5yd). Fold this strip in half lengthways, with right sides together and stitch close to the raw edges. Turn strip right sides out and press with the seam running centrally on the underside. This will be the back of the ruffle. Make a line of gathering stitches down the centre of the ruffle and pull up to fit around the quilt along the raw seam. Tack (baste) ruffle in place and using three strands of embroidery thread, work a line of chain-stitch over the gathering, to hold it in place and make a decorative finish.

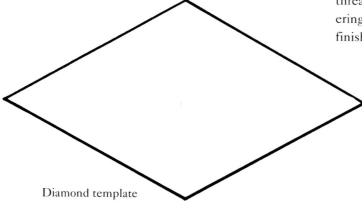

Diamond template

Chain-stitch

Sewing Casket
with Patchwork Lid

Sewing caskets were very popular throughout the nineteenth century. They were usually a four-sided box rather than five sides, as I have designed here (see page 18), and were made in various sizes from very tiny ones, which were possibly toys, to rather splendid ones, that could be displayed on a side table. The idea was to hold all the necessary items for sewing in one container and to display them attractively when the lid was removed as shown below.

Thick card
Pieces of thin card for lining
50cm (½yd) of the main fabric
Scraps of similar fabric in five toning patterns for
  the patchwork lid
Matching threads
Plain lining fabric (lawn or silk is ideal)
Purchased tassel and cord in toning colour
  or DMC coton perlé to make your own
Narrow satin ribbon in two toning colours
Scraps of thin wadding
A pencil, cut to 6.5cm (2½in) long
Cartridge paper
PVA glue
Sharp craft knife and ruler
Needlework items: scissors, various pins and needles,
  tape measure, needle threader, bodkins, safety pins,
  thimble and a long reel of white thread

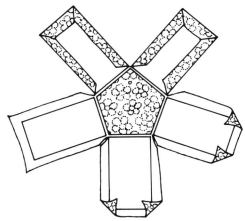
Layout for box sides and base

❶ Start by drawing out the full-size pattern for the box sides, base, inner box, lid and sides. Use this to cut out five side pieces, one base, one lid-top, five lid side pieces, one inner base and five inner side pieces from thick card. Cut a round hole, as marked, in the centre of the inner base piece.

❷ Cut a piece of the main fabric, a little larger all round than the box base. Lay this, right side down, on the work surface and place the card base centrally on top. Fold the edges of the fabric round on to the back of the card and glue in place.

❸ Cut out a piece of the main fabric 35cm (14in) square. Lay this, right side down, on your work surface and glue the covered box base in the centre, right side uppermost. Place the box sides round the base, matching up the sides of the pentagonal base with each side piece and leaving a small gap in between. This gap should be about the thickness of the card. Carefully trim the fabric round the card pieces to leave about 2.5cm (1in) excess all round. Fold over the excess fabric and glue to the card. Snip the excess fabric to make it lie flat.

❹ Cut out five pieces of thin card slightly smaller than the box sides. Glue a piece of the wadding to one side of each piece and trim the wadding flush with the edge of the card. Lay each piece of card, wadding side down, on to the wrong side of a piece of the lining fabric. Bring the raw edges of the fabric round and glue them to the back of the card.

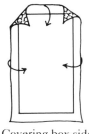
Covering box side

❺ Cut five 8cm (3in) pieces from each of the two ribbons. Glue one of each colour round the card lining pieces. Now glue the lining pieces to the box sides so that all the raw fabric edges are hidden.

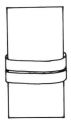
Adding ribbons

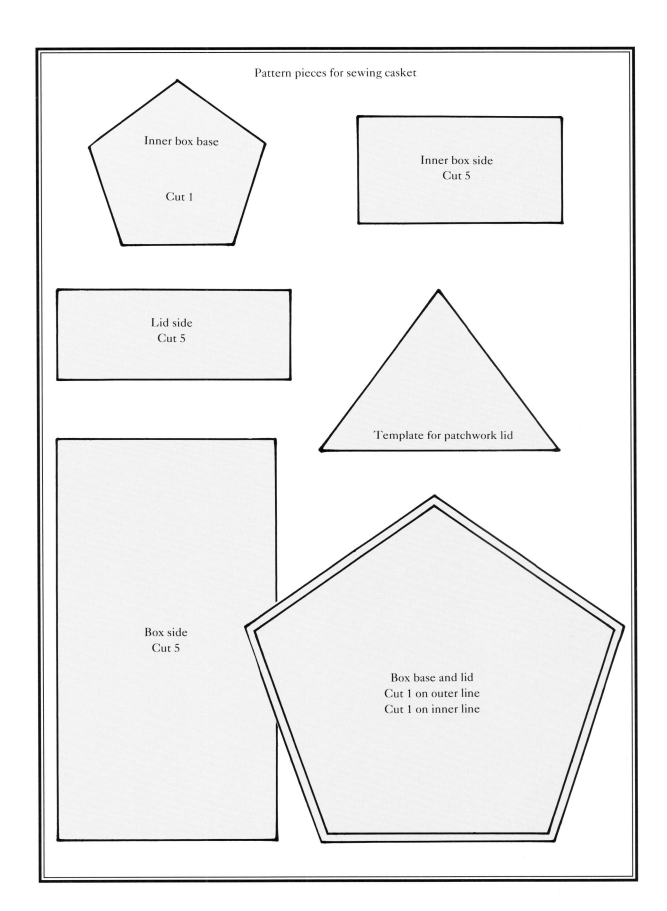

Pattern pieces for sewing casket

Inner box base

Cut 1

Inner box side
Cut 5

Lid side
Cut 5

Template for patchwork lid

Box side
Cut 5

Box base and lid
Cut 1 on outer line
Cut 1 on inner line

❻ Make up the small inner box in exactly the same way but omit the ribbon. Snip the fabric inside the hole in the base and glue the points to the underside of the card. Cover the pencil by gluing on a strip of the main fabric, leaving 2.5cm (1in) of fabric free at the bottom end. Push the covered pencil up through the hole in the base. Snip the excess fabric at the end of the pencil and glue the fabric under the card base, to hold the pencil firmly. Now glue the base of the inner box centrally to the base of the main box. The points of the small pentagons should match up with the centres of the sides on the large pentagon, so that the box falls open correctly.

Gluing pencil to base

Keep your sewing casket handy for all those little last-minute sewing jobs.

❼ To cover the lid, cut out a piece of the main fabric 35 × 5cm (14 × 2in). Lay it out on the work surface, right side down. Place the lid sides, in a line, centrally along the fabric, leaving a tiny gap between each piece. Fold the excess fabric, along one long side, over the card and glue in place. Glue the fabric over one short end. Fold this strip to fit round the edge of the lid top. Bring the excess fabric on to the lid top and glue to the card to hold in place. Cut out slightly smaller pieces of thin card to fit inside the lid, cover them with lining fabric and glue in place.

Assembling the lid

❽ To make the patchwork top for the lid, cut out five triangles in cartridge paper from the pattern. Pin these to the wrong side of the five scraps of patchwork fabric and tack (baste) in place folding in the corners as you go. Remove the pins. Carefully slipstitch the triangles together to form the pentagon shape. Remove the tacking (basting) threads and the patchwork papers. Cut out a lid-top in thin card and glue on a layer of wadding. Cover this with the patchwork, matching up the base of each triangle with the sides of the pentagon. Glue the patchwork fabric to the back of the card.

❾ Take the tassel and stitch it through the centre of the patchwork lid-top. You could of course make your own stitched-head tassel as shown in the Tassels and Cords chapter. Glue the lid-top in place, to cover all the raw edges of fabric.

❿ Put the reel of thread over the pencil and place the thimble on top. Push various pins and needles into the flaps of the inner box and insert all the remaining needlework items under the ribbons on the box sides. Bring up the sides and place the lid on top to close.

Quilted Bedroom Accessories

These luxurious satin accessories (page 21) are worked by hand using traditional English quilting. The cushion and nightdress case look lovely displayed on top of the bed, and the drawstring bag is a perfect place to keep delicate stockings and underwear.

❶ Trace off the design from the book, using a fine black waterproof felt-tipped pen. Tape the satin fabric over the tracing and draw over the design using a soluble felt-tipped embroidery marker pen, or a white chalk quilting pencil. It is best to test the marker pen on some spare fabric first to make sure that it will wash out.

❷ The quilted areas for each article should be stitched first and then the pieces can be made up into the finished items. Cut out the satin fabric, wadding and backing to the required shape and tack (baste) them together carefully before you begin quilting. This is a very important stage in quilting, as the layers can easily slip out of place as you are stitching. The wadding should be laid between the layers of fabric and the right sides of the fabric should be on the outside. Use a fine needle and thread, so as not to mark the satin unnecessarily, and start tacking (basting) with a knot on the right side. Start stitching in the centre of the fabric and work out towards the corners. Then tack (baste) vertically and horizontally in lines about 10cm (4in) apart. Lastly tack (baste) all round the

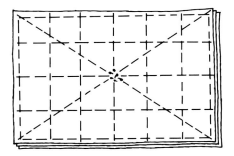
Tacking (basting) fabric layers in place

fabric near the raw edge. Work with medium-length stitches, not pulled too tightly.

❸ Most small pieces of work can be hand quilted without the need for an embroidery frame but some people find it easier to use a frame as it keeps the backing fabric taut, allowing the quilting to show up well on the surface.

❹ You can use either matching silk thread or special, stronger quilting thread for your stitching. Begin in the centre of the design and work outwards, to keep the layers even. Use a fine quilting needle and make small, even running stitches. The smaller and more detailed the pattern, the smaller and closer together these stitches should be. Fasten off securely on the reverse with two or three backstitches.

Cushion

35cm (14in) square cushion pad
50cm (½yd) peach satin
46cm (18in) square of medium-weight polyester wadding
Matching thread
46cm (18in) square of backing fabric

❶ Cut out two 46cm (18in) squares of peach satin. Fold one piece of satin in half and mark along the fold. Open it out and fold in half the other way and mark again. This is to mark the centre of the cushion front.

❷ Trace off the quarter pattern on page 20.

Draw the quilting lines through on to the centre of the satin, turning the tracing over twice to complete the whole pattern.

Tack (baste) the satin, wadding and backing together, as described on page 19, and hand quilt along the pattern lines by working small running stitches.

❸ For the frill, cut and join 9cm (3½in) wide pieces of satin to make a strip 3m (3¼yd) long. Fold the strip in half lengthways, with the right side outside. Run a gathering thread 1.5cm (⅝in) from the raw edge. Pull up the gathers to fit round the cushion front. Pin and tack (baste) the frill in place, matching up the raw edges. Tuck in the short raw ends to neaten. Machine stitch frill in place.

❹ Lay the satin cushion back on top, with right sides together, and tack (baste) all round. Machine stitch over the first row of stitches, leaving a 25cm (10in) gap along one side for

Centre point

¼ pattern for cushion

Add seam allowance

Add seam allowance

turning. Trim the excess fabric at the corners and turn right sides out. Carefully remove all the rows of tacking (basting), pulling them out by the knots.

❺ Insert the cushion pad and hand stitch the opening to neaten. You could insert a light-weight zip here to make removal of the cover easier for cleaning.

NIGHTDRESS CASE

70cm (¾yd) each of pale peach satin, medium-weight polyester wadding and backing fabric
Matching thread
Tiny matching ribbon bow
Press fastener

❶ Following the diagram, cut out satin, wadding and backing fabric for the front and back of the nightdress case. Mark on the quilting patterns and tack (baste) the layers together for each piece. Hand stitch all the quilting.

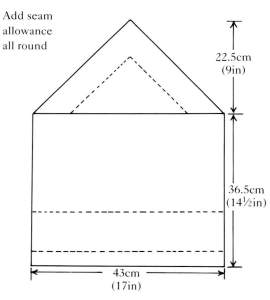

Add seam allowance all round

22.5cm (9in)

36.5cm (14½in)

43cm (17in)

Pattern pieces for nightdress case

❷ Cut out a 79 × 6cm (31 × 2½in) bias strip of satin. Use this to bind the raw edges of the pointed flap of the nightdress case. Make a small pleat at the point to make the fabric lie flat.

❸ Place the quilted front piece over the back piece, with right sides together and raw edges matching. Machine stitch the sides and lower edge, taking a 1.5cm (⅝in) seam. Trim away the wadding and the backing fabric close to the seam. Fold the satin fabric seam allowance over, to cover the raw edges of the seam, and hand stitch to neaten. Remove all the tacking.

❹ Turn the case right sides out and sew on a press fastener and a tiny bow at the point of the flap to complete.

DRAWSTRING BAG

50cm (½yd) each of pale peach satin, backing fabric and medium-weight polyester wadding
Matching thread
1m (1yd) of matching silky cord

❶ Mark the border pattern along one long edge of the satin. Following the diagram, cut out the bag to size and tack (baste) the layers together as before. Hand quilt along the marked lines.

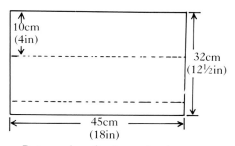

10cm (4in)

32cm (12½in)

45cm (18in)

Pattern piece for drawstring bag

❷ Fold the quilted fabric in half, with right sides together, so that the short sides are level. Machine stitch 1.5cm (⅝in) from the raw edge to make a tube. Neaten the seam as for the night-dress case and turn right side out. Thread a needle with double thread and make a line of gathering stitches close to the lower raw edge. Pull up these stitches tightly and tie the threads securely.

❸ Cut out a 10cm (4in) diameter circle of satin and another from the backing fabric. Run a gathering thread round the edge of each circle.

Pull up the gathers slightly to make the raw edge of the circle fold under to the wrong side. Fasten the threads securely. Press the circles flat and hand stitch the satin circle centrally to the base of the bag on the outside. Stitch the other one to the inside to neaten.

❹ Cut out a strip of satin 45 × 11cm (18 × 4½in) to fit along the top of the bag. With right sides together, stitch the strip along the top of the bag, folding under the short raw ends to neaten. Fold this piece over to the inside to enclose the raw top edge and fold under and hand stitch the other edge to the inside of the bag.

Stitch a channel 3cm (1¼in) away from the fold. Where the short ends overlap, insert the silky cord into the channel to close the bag. Knot the ends of the cord and tease out the ends to form tassels. Remove all the tacking (basting) stitches to finish.

Actual-size pattern for nightdress case and drawstring bag

Repeat pattern

Crazy Patchwork Throw

Crazy patchwork consists of irregular-shaped patches hand stitched on to a backing fabric. No templates or patchwork papers are needed, and there is no necessity for careful measuring or working out of patterns. The whole effect is delightfully rich and random with the added attraction of decorative embroidery outlining each patch.

Crazy patchwork was a very thrifty type of needlework as off-cuts from clothing and furnishings were the ideal fabrics. A mixture of velvets, silk, brocade, heavy satin, woollens and furnishing cotton is typical. In fact all the fabrics that were not suitable for the more intricate forms of patchwork could be used in this way. It was not usually padded or quilted but the warmth came from the use of heavier material and the addition of backing fabric.

This crazy patchwork throw can be made to any size you wish and used as a decorative addition to a plain sofa. A smaller piece would be perfect as a small cloth or rug.

An assortment of plain and patterned fabrics in varied weights and toning colours
Calico or sheeting for backing
Fabric for edging the patchwork
Matching threads
Stranded embroidery cotton in toning colour
Crewel needle

---

❶ Begin by cutting up some of the fabrics into random shapes. Lay these out on to the backing fabric and pin in place temporarily to make a good arrangement of colours, shapes and sizes. Start near one corner of the backing fabric and sew on the first patch, using matching thread and tiny running stitches, close to the raw edge. Lay the next patch in place, slightly overlapping the first patch and stitch in the same way. Turn under the overlapping edge if necessary.

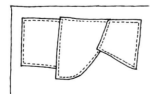

Working crazy patchwork

❷ Fabrics that fray easily will need to have their edges turned under before stitching to the backing. Velvet, however, is too bulky to do this so make sure that all the raw edges on these patches are covered by the surrounding pieces.

❸ Continue in this way until the backing fabric is covered, apart from a border 8cm (3in) wide all round. Using three strands of the embroidery cotton, work a traditional feather stitch or herringbone stitch over the joins of all the patches. This will cover the running stitches and also add extra decoration. Choose a strong colour that will pull the whole composition together. Victorian ladies sometimes added more embroidery and even beadwork to plain patches.

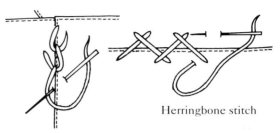

Herringbone stitch

Feather stitch

❹ To complete the throw, you will need to add a border. Choose a fabric from the patchwork, if you have enough, or select a different one that will show off the rich collection of colours and designs. Cut out strips of the border fabric 18cm (7in) wide and 15cm (6in) longer than each side of the backing fabric. With right sides together, pin and tack the border pieces centrally on to the patchwork, so that the raw edges of the patches match up with the raw edges of the border fabric. Where the border pieces meet, at the corners, mitre the ends neatly and trim away any excess fabric. Machine stitch in place.

❺ Fold half the border over to the back of the throw, turn under the raw edges and slipstitch neatly to the back. To hide the stitching on the back of the throw and to add extra warmth, you could add another layer of fabric over the back before slipstitching the border in place.

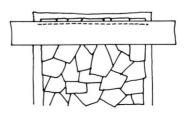

Adding border strips

Patchwork Star

Stars like this were made as pincushions or, because they have sixty diamond-shaped pieces, to commemorate Queen Victoria's sixty years on the throne. Each star is built up of cardboard shapes covered in fabric and meticulously stitched together by hand. The points and centres are then further embellished with beads.

Scraps of toning floral lawn in at least five different
  patterns
Matching threads
Thin card
PVA glue
Beads, sequins and ribbon to decorate
Sharp craft knife, cutting board and ruler

❶ Trace off the diamond shape and use it to cut out sixty accurate templates from the thin card. Roughly cut out slightly larger, diamond-shaped pieces from your fabrics. Lay the fabric right side down on the work surface and place a card diamond in the centre. Fold the edges of the fabric over the edge of the card and glue to the back.

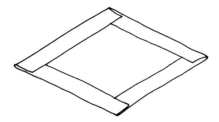

Gluing fabric to card diamond

❷ Assemble the covered diamonds in groups of five, each one in a different pattern. Take two of the diamonds and place them together, with right sides facing. With tiny oversewing stitches, join the diamonds together, along one side. Open them out flat and lay another diamond on top of the second diamond. Join these two in the same way, so that the stitching meets at the point. Continue in this way until you have joined all five diamonds into a star. Try to keep the stitching as small as possible, so that it hardly shows on the right side. Stitch a small bead into the centre of the star. Repeat with all the other diamonds to make twelve stars.

This patchwork star is made in floral lawn patches trimmed with beads and ribbon bows. Hung well out of reach, it would make a delightful mobile for a baby's nursery.

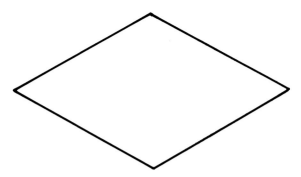

Diamond template

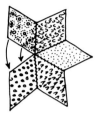

Stitching diamonds into a star

❸ Now stitch the individual stars together. To do this you have to stitch on the right side. Take the first star and join it to the second, by stitching the sides of two of the diamonds together. Stitch the third star in place, joining it to the first star and then to the second. Join the fourth star to the first and third stars and so on until you have completed half the star. Try to arrange the patchwork so that no two similar patterns are next to each other. Make the other half of the star in the same way.

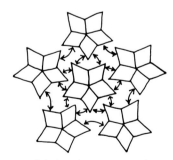

Joining the stars together

❹ Stitch a sequin, a large and a tiny bead on to each point of the star. Thread ribbon loops through the top and base of the star, for hanging and decoration. Then fit the two halves of the star together and stitch them in place to complete.

Flowercraft

Pressed Flowers

Pressing flowers is probably one of the first crafts a child can learn and it is also something that an accomplished crafts person can take delight in. How enjoyable to gather a few flowers on a country walk or from a favourite garden, press them between the leaves of a large old book and then make them into a lovely card or picture, to remind you of a special day. You don't need any expensive equipment or great artistic skills to achieve some really lovely results.

HOW TO PRESS FLOWERS

A large heavy book or a flower press
Sheets of clean blotting paper

❶ Collect the flowers on a dry day after any dew has dried. Select several of the same type of blooms, together with a few buds and small pieces of foliage. The most successful flowers to press are ones that grow fairly flat on the plant and so do not become too distorted when pressed. Yellow, mauve and blue flowers keep their colour best, but it is still worth trying pink and red ones, even though they tend to discolour after a while.

❷ Carefully cut the flowers from the stems and leaves and lay them out on a sheet of folded blotting paper. Arrange the blooms on the sheet leaving space for them to flatten out. Press the foliage and stems on another sheet. Fold the blotting paper over to enclose the plants and put them between the leaves of the book. Pile more books on top to weight it down and then leave for about three weeks to dry out. Check after this time, carefully opening the blotting paper so as not to tear the fragile petals. If the flowers are papery and flat and they come away from the blotting paper easily, then they are ready, but they may need another week or two to dry out before you can use them safely.

GREETINGS CARDS

Card or paper
PVA glue
Tweezers
Watercolour brushes
Ready-made card mounts or pieces of card to cut yourself
Transparent adhesive film
Finger-plate
Frames

❶ For greetings cards, you can use ready-made card mounts and protect the arrangement with transparent adhesive film. Otherwise you can use white or coloured card and cut and fold the card yourself. When using the ready-made window mounts, trace the shape of the mount very lightly, with a pencil, on to the backing piece.

❷ Open the card out flat and make your arrangement within this area. Pick up the flowers with tweezers and move them about with a dry brush. When you are happy with the design, lift a petal here and there and dab a little glue underneath, to hold it in position. Cut out a piece of the transparent film, slightly larger than the area indicated by the pencil line. Very gently rub away the pencil mark and cover the whole arrangement with the film. Press it down

carefully to exclude any air bubbles. Now fold the mount over the flowers to complete.

❸ When you are making your own cards try to cut them out so that they fit standard-sized envelopes. Make the cards in the same way but glue the flowers down more firmly and omit the film. You can make gift tags in the same way and add a loop of ribbon to tie to the parcel. You

Press flowers and leaves throughout the year to give a good choice of colours and shapes.

can also use the designs from existing cards, by cutting out the picture, mounting it on to a larger sheet of thin card and decorating the mount with an arrangement of pressed flowers.

PICTURES

❶ To make pressed flower pictures, remove the glass from the frame and use this as a guide to cut out a piece of card to fit into your frame. Either work with this card in the frame or draw a light pencil line to indicate the area you can work in.

❷ For the round picture, begin at the outer edge with a circle of delicate foliage. Then glue on a circle of pink larkspur, some plain leaves and a circle of blue delphinium petals. Finish in the centre with a dark flower. The whole picture looks like a typical Victorian posy as seen from above. Finally replace the glass in the frame, making sure it is really clean and then put in your arrangement. Add several pieces of backing card, to make sure the flowers are pressed firmly up against the glass and to help hold all the tiny pieces in place. Then use small panel pins, knocked in around the edge, to hold everything in the frame securely.

Decorate a plain finger-plate with an arrangement of pressed flowers to suit the room.

Pressed flowers, marbled paper and pretty scraps all go together to make these delightful cards, pictures and lampshade.

❸ Make the design for the oval frame in the same way as for the cards, massing the flower heads together and adding a few silvery leaves. Cut an oval mount in marbled paper to set off the arrangement. Assemble in the frame as for the round picture.

FINGER-PLATE

To make the finger-plate, you will need a completely plain, clear plastic or glass finger-plate. Trace round it on to a piece of paper and cut the shape out in transparent adhesive film. Lay the flowers, face down, on to the back of the finger-plate. Lift the plate very carefully every now and then, to check your design from the front. When you are happy with it, peel off the backing paper and spread the film over the back of the finger-plate to adhere the flowers to the glass or plastic. Press carefully to exclude any air bubbles. You may need to pierce any obstinate bubbles with a pin and push out the air before you screw the finger-plate to the door.

LAMPSHADE

For the lampshade I used a selection of small, prettily shaped autumn leaves. These press very successfully and retain their beautiful colours. Use a plain, pale coloured shade so that the colours will show up when the lamp is lit, as well as in the daytime. Try out the leaves, holding up one or two at a time to estimate their positions. Then paint a thin layer of glue all over the back of each leaf and press it on to the shade. Work all the way round in this way. You will need to glue these leaves on more securely than the flowers as they are going on to a curved surface and will suffer more wear and tear. You will find that the shade is very quick to make and looks delightful.

Dried Flowers

In winter time, when fresh flowers were at a premium, the Victorian head gardener was still expected to come up with numerous floral displays to decorate the big house. To add to his pot plants and flowers from the greenhouse, he usually had a good supply of dried garden flowers at hand. These were picked at the height of the summer and dried in airy garden sheds, in the warm weather. Favourite flowers were rose-buds, peonies, lavender, statice and helichrysum. Sometimes they were embellished by being dipped into a solution of alum, to make the petals sparkle. Even drops of essential oil were sprinkled on to an arrangement to make it smell sweet. These displays were often covered by glass domes to keep off the ever-present dust from coal fires, and to preserve them even longer. In fact a few displays are still in existence today, although they do look rather faded.

TO DRY FLOWERS

Fresh flowers picked just before their prime, such as peonies, rose-buds, hydrangeas, statice, larkspur and lavender
String
Hooks or a clothes airer
Flower wires and a wire cutter
Gutta percha or florist's wrap
Cone-shaped Styrofoam blocks
White paper posy holders or doilies
Glass domes, old, or modern copies

---

❶ Pick your blooms in the summer months, at the height of their season. Choose a warm, dry day and select flowers that are not quite in full bloom, as they will continue to develop slightly while they are drying. Experiment with different flowers and you will soon find the perfect moment to pick each type of plant, so that it dries looking its best. Rose-buds are a little more flexible, regarding the precise moment of picking. But try to choose ones where the colour of the petals is quite obvious and the green sepals have opened and drawn back. All sorts of garden roses are suitable, as are the typical pink and red rose-buds you can buy in florists. In fact I think these are better dried, as they seldom seem to come into bloom successfully when arranged in water. Tiny wild rose-buds also dry very well and are perfect for a miniature posy or the top-most flowers in a small display.

❷ To supplement your own collection of dried flowers you can also buy ready-dried ones and silk flowers with slightly browned edges that look very Victorian.

❸ To dry your own flowers, strip off most, or all, of the leaves and hang them up in groups of about five, depending on the size of the flower. Large peonies are best hung singly as the blooms easily get squashed out of shape and

---

Show off your dried flowers for years to come under beautiful glass domes.

This quick and easy arrangement is set in a pretty creamware basket. The flower stems are simply pushed into a Styrofoam block hidden in the basket.

---

then dry like that. Tie the stems loosely with string and suspend them near the ceiling of a warm airy room. An old-fashioned clothes airer is perfect for this purpose. Flowers hung above an Aga cooking range dry very quickly and successfully too.

❹ Touch is the best way to tell when your flowers are ready. They should feel quite dry and papery, with hard and brittle stems.

❺ Each type of flower will take a different drying time and this will also vary with the atmosphere in your drying room. Leave them until all the flowers for one display are ready and then prepare them for arranging.

❻ It is best to cut the flower stems fairly short, so that they do not snap when you push them into the Styrofoam blocks. If you need extra length for your arrangement, cut a piece of stiff floral wire and push it up inside the hollow stem. If the stem is solid or too narrow for this, lay the wire alongside the stem and then bind it in place, with fine wire, to hold it securely. Cover this with green or brown gutta percha or florist's wrap to hide the wire.

GLASS-DOMED ARRANGEMENTS

Mass the flowers close together to form a traditional posy shape.

❶ Using a sharp kitchen knife, cut the cone-shaped Styrofoam block to the required shape so that it fits easily under your dome and allows space for the flowers. Cut out the centre of a paper posy holder or doily and slip this over the Styrofoam cone, pulling it down to the base.

Slip the doily over the cone

❷ Start arranging your flowers at the bottom of the cone, working in circles of the same flower type, gradually building up to the point. Generally it is best to have the larger flowers near the base and grade them in size towards the top. Fill in the spaces between big roses or peony flowers with clusters of lavender or sprigs of statice. Choose one perfect flower or bud for the top of the arrangement. Try the glass dome over the flowers and make any adjustments necessary. Cover the base of the dome with pretty fabric, paper or a doily to finish off.

Needlepoint

Needlepoint

Needlepoint (or canvas work) was at the height of its popularity in the middle of Queen Victoria's reign. Women from the upper and middle classes made many lovely items for their homes, from large carpets and sets of dining chair seats to tiny pincushions and even slippers. The photograph on the previous page shows a selection of original Victorian pieces.

The brilliant colours that the Victorians loved look rather garish to our eyes nowadays, so the designs I have chosen for this chapter are worked in the more subtle, muted shades that we expect when we think of the Victorian style. All the projects are stitched in traditional half cross stitch, tent stitch or basketweave tent stitch, which all appear the same from the front and are quick and easy to work. Half cross stitch is the most economical but it tends to pull the canvas diagonally out of shape.

Tent stitch is also easy to do, but because it makes a longer diagonal on the back of the work it uses more wool. It also distorts the canvas. Basketweave tent stitch causes the least distortion and is ideal for the larger background areas. You can use a combination of stitching methods to suit the size of area to be worked.

Each project has its own instructions but these general notes will be especially useful to beginners.

CANVAS

In each project I have suggested the type and size of canvas to use but you can enlarge or reduce the size of the piece slightly, depending on the gauge of the canvas that is available. I prefer to work on a double-thread canvas as it is softer to hold whilst working and also easier when making up the finished piece into the more complex articles. Single-thread canvas is also good and sometimes more easily available.

White canvas is preferable for light coloured pieces but you can get natural and dark coloured meshes which are ideal if you have a large amount of dark background. When working on larger mesh canvas it helps to buy canvas as close as possible to the colour of the background wool.

YARNS

Always choose good quality tapestry wools (yarns) and buy the whole amount needed at one time as slight colour variations sometimes occur.

Use one strand of 4-ply tapestry wool or three or four strands of the finer crewel wool, if preferred. Personally I prefer the tapestry wool, as I find it much easier to thread into the needle.

STITCHING

Cut your wool (yarn) into manageable lengths. About 75cm (30in) is ideal as you don't have to re-thread the needle too often and the wool does not fray from continually being pulled through the canvas.

Begin by bringing the wool up from the underside of the canvas. Leave about 5cm (2in) of wool at the back and hold this in place while you make the first few stitches over it, to stop the stitching coming undone. Work the stitches, following the diagram for your chosen stitch and finish off the thread by weaving it behind two or three stitches and then cutting off the end to leave about 5cm (2in) of wool. This can be

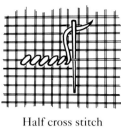

Half cross stitch

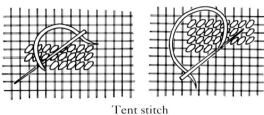

Tent stitch

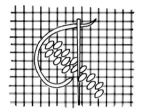

Basketweave tent stitch

incorporated in the back of the work as you go. You can move to another area of the same colour without fastening off the wool but the next area should be a maximum distance of 2cm (¾in) away. If you try to carry the wool any further, there will be too many strands criss-crossing the back of the work and the finished result will suffer. Try to keep the stitch tension regular. You should aim for a smooth even look, where the wool is not so tight that the canvas shows through nor so loose that loops form on the front.

WORKING FROM THE CHARTS

Generally, it is best to start stitching in the centre of the design and work out towards the edge, finishing with the background. This is the best way to use a charted design to avoid making mistakes in counting the squares. You should always mark the centre of the canvas, both vertically and horizontally, with a line of tacking (basting) to match the centre lines on the charts. (Never use pencil, which will discolour the wool.)

Remember that each square on the chart represents one stitch on the needlepoint. You may find this confusing at first as the lines on the chart look like the threads of the canvas but they should not be read as such. The easiest way to clarify this is to count the squares on the chart and count the threads on the canvas.

STRETCHING

Most finished needlepoint will need stretching to give a good final result. You will need a large piece of blockboard, a set square and ruler, a plant spray, several sheets of clean white blotting paper and good quality drawing pins or staple gun.

Start by spraying the back of your needlepoint with water so that is very damp but not soaking wet. Lay the sheets of blotting paper out on the blockboard and spray them lightly with water. Place the needlepoint face down on the blotting paper and pull it into shape with your hands. You may have to pull quite strongly and then check the accuracy with the set square and ruler. Pin or staple along one edge, through the canvas only, stretching it as you go. Now pin the opposite edge, pulling it really taut. Pin the other two sides in the same way, starting at the centre point on each side and working out towards the corners. Lightly spray the whole surface of the needlepoint and then leave it in a warm place to dry gently over one or two days. Do not be tempted to dry it too fast against a radiator or you may damage all your hard work. When it is quite dry and flat, remove the pins or staples and make it up into your finished item. Sometimes you may need to repeat this process if your work is very badly distorted.

Pinning work to board

Floral Footstool

All-over designs and repeating patterns are a most versatile type of needlepoint work. The beauty of these designs is that they can be used in large areas to fit all sorts of projects like dining chair seats, footstools, ottomans, fire-screens and cushions.

This type of design is less demanding than a complex motif such as a floral bouquet, as you soon get used to the pattern and can work it without constant reference to the chart. The skeleton of the design can be stitched first, leaving the rest to be filled in at your leisure.

Any shape of furniture can be accommodated, by simply drawing out an accurate pattern of your chair seat, curtain tie-back or box top and transferring this to the canvas with tacking (basting) stitches. Plan the design so that it falls centrally within the shape and begin stitching from the centre, working outwards to the tacking (basting) stitches. Decorative borders worked in the same colours as the all-over pattern look very effective as an edging with this sort of project especially on a rectangular cushion or fire-screen.

This rather abstract floral design is typical of patterns from the mid-nineteenth century. It comes from the design archives of the Royal School of Needlework and was originally stitched in bright reds and orange with naturalistic bright green leaves and a very pale background. Over the years the colours have faded into what we now think of as the typical Victorian look, so to echo this I have chosen muted mauves and violets for the flowers with a bland putty-coloured background to set it off.

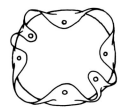

Pinning canvas to round pad

For a circular footstool 28cm (11in) diameter:

Double-thread tapestry canvas 11 holes to 2.5cm
(1in), 10cm (4in) larger than your footstool pad
Tapestry frame or carpet tape
Appletons tapestry wools (yarns) as follows:
8 skeins of 984, 4 skeins each of 602 and 606,
3 skeins each of 604 and 241, 2 skeins
each of 645 and 243, 1 skein of 695
Size 24 tapestry needle
A staple gun or tacks and a hammer

❶ Start the needlepoint by binding the edge of the canvas with tape, or mounting it on to a frame. Mark the centre point of the canvas and the outer edge with tacking (basting) stitches. The whole design is worked in half cross or tent stitch.

❷ Begin stitching at the centre point of the canvas with the centre of one flower. Then work outwards to the edge of the flower and stitch the bud. Carefully count to the next flower centre and work in the same way all over the required area. Then stitch the stems and leaves and lastly fill in the background colour.

❸ Stretch the needlepoint as described on page 41. Lay the canvas over the footstool pad and pin in place at the centre point. Turn the pad over, pull the canvas round and staple to the back. Staple first at the top and bottom, then at both sides and then between these points, pulling the canvas taut, making pleats as small as possible. Trim away any excess canvas and then screw the padded top in place on to the footstool base.

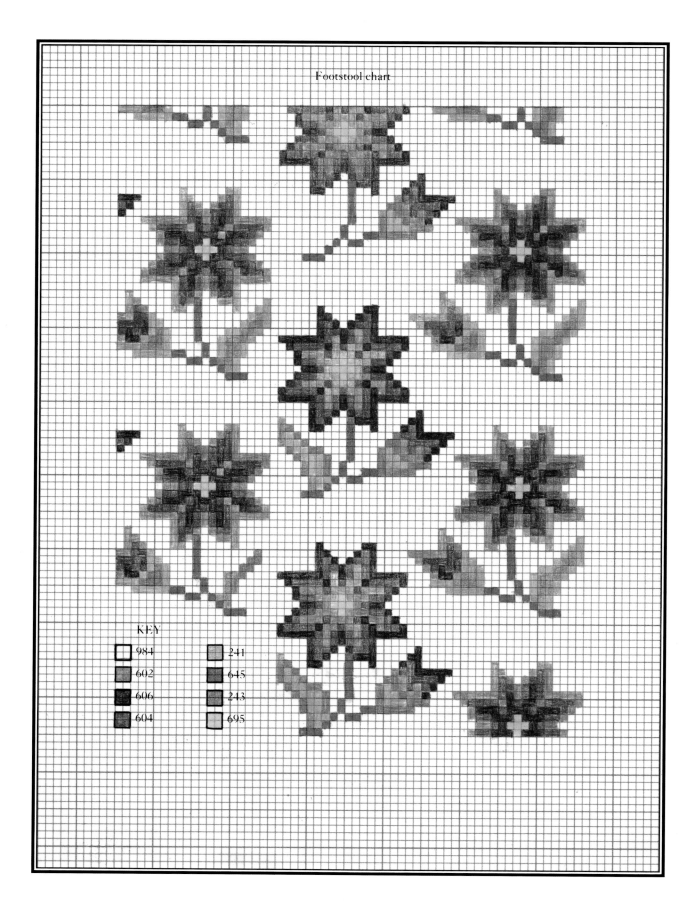

Footstool chart

KEY
984
602
606
604
241
645
243
695

Posy picture chart

KEY

	703		561
	405		921
	562		154
	463		251
	464		544

	403
	756		831
	757		647
	208		991
	206		941
	475		944

Victorian Posy

This delightful posy was inspired by the Victorian greetings card
shown opposite. Shown here mounted as a picture, the design could
also be used for a chair seat or cushion.

*60 × 50cm (24 × 20in) double-thread tapestry
   canvas, 12 holes to 2.5cm (1in)*
Appletons tapestry wools (yarns) as follows:
   *3 skeins of 703, 2 skeins of 405, 1 skein each of
   562, 463, 464, 561, 921, 154, 251, 544, 403,
   831, 647, 991, 941, 944, 756, 757, 208, 206,
   475*
Size 24 tapestry needle
*Oval frame with internal measurements 35 × 28cm
   (13¾ × 11in)*
Tapestry frame or carpet tape
Darning needle and strong linen thread

❶ Start the needlepoint by binding the edge of the canvas with tape, or mounting it on to a frame. Mark the centre of the design vertically and horizontally with tacking (basting) stitches. The whole design is worked in half cross or tent stitch. (See chart, page 45.)

❷ Begin stitching in the central area, working the large rose in the five different colours. Count out from the marked lines to help you position the flower correctly.

When the first flower is complete, it will be relatively easy to work outwards from the edge of these petals in all directions. Stitch whole leaves, buds and flowers as complete areas. This will save changing wools (yarns) too often and help to keep a sense of achievement as you finish each section.

❸ When you reach the edge of the design you can begin to stitch rows of the background colour. This is a much more restful part of the work and it is a good idea to stitch the background at night when the light is not so good and you may be relaxing or watching television at the same time.

❹ The amount of background will depend on how you are going to use the finished needle-point. If you want to make a panelled cushion, work out an oval or rectangular border to fit comfortably round the design and work up to this. The outer border can be more needlepoint

worked in different coloured wools, or you could make up a velvet or brocade edging which will speed up the process greatly. The corners should be mitred, to make the fabric lie flat and you could add stitched-on braid to complete the effect.

❺ When you have finished the stitching, stretch the canvas, as described on page 41. If you are making the picture, you will need to mount the canvas on to a piece of thick board that has been cut slightly undersize to fit loosely into the frame. This will allow for the extra canvas folded around the edge. The stitching can stop about 5mm (¼in) from the edge as this will be hidden under the frame rebate.

❻ Position the design centrally on the board and then turn it over carefully so that the needlepoint is face down. Insert pins into the edge of the board to hold it in place. Using a darning needle and strong linen thread, lace the canvas round the board. Work across the centre vertically and horizontally then diagonally, pulling the canvas evenly. Lift and check the front of the work occasionally to make sure the design has not been pulled out of place. Remove the pins as you go.

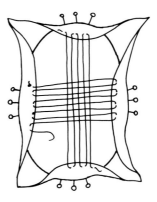

Lacing canvas on oval board

Ring o' Roses Pincushion

The design for this elegant pincushion was taken from a set of antique lace dressing-table mats, with the roses embroidered in silk, which translated well into needlepoint.

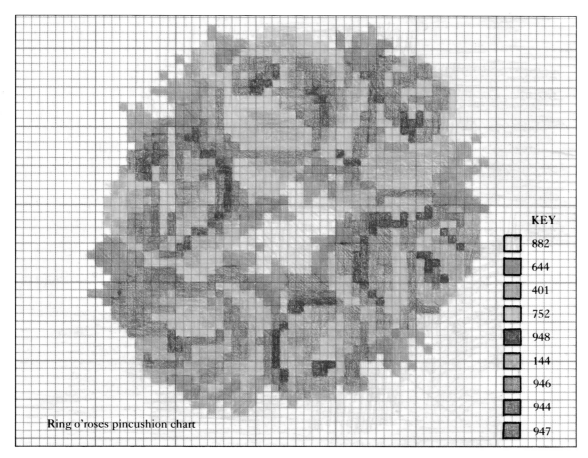

KEY

☐	882
☐	644
☐	401
☐	752
☐	948
☐	144
☐	946
☐	944
☐	947

Ring o'roses pincushion chart

20cm (8in) square of tapestry canvas, 13 holes to 2.5cm (1in)
Appletons tapestry wools (yarns) as follows:
  2 skeins of 882, 1 skein each of 644, 401, 752, 948, 144, 946, 944, 947
Size 24 tapestry needle
11cm (4¼in) diameter pincushion base or a 13cm (5in) square of velvet for backing the cushion, and wadding

❶ Begin by binding the canvas edge with tape, or mounting it into a frame. The design is worked in half cross or tent stitch.

❷ Mark the centre of your canvas vertically and horizontally with lines of tacking. Count out from the centre of the chart and begin by stitching one rose at a time. It is quite a detailed chart with lots of colours so try not to have too many ends of wool looping across as this makes the back of the work very lumpy.

❸ When you have finished the circle of roses, fill in the foliage and then stitch the background. To gauge the amount of background area you need to work, lay the needlepoint over the padded pincushion base and mark the canvas with a few tacking (basting) stitches around the edge of the base. Do the same to make a square cushion, making sure that the design is in the centre each time. The ideal finished size for the square pincushion would be about 11.5cm (4½in).

❹ When you have finished the needlepoint, stretch the canvas as described in Stretching (see page 41) ready for making up the pincushion. To make the round pincushion, follow the instructions for finishing the footstool (page 42). For a square pincushion, follow the instructions for the trellis cushion (page 50) and then stuff it firmly with scraps of wadding before sewing up the gap to neaten.

Trellis Cushion with Tassels

The all-over design on this smart cushion has a more masculine flavour and is slightly more complex than the floral pattern on the previous pages. I have adapted it from an original Victorian pattern that was meant for gentlemen's carpet slippers. Because it is small, the cushion is ideal as a first-time project, or use the design on drop-in dining chair seats. It could be worked in either very pretty colours to suit a bedroom or strongly contrasting shades that would go well in a modern sitting room.

For a 35cm (14in) square cushion you will need:

45cm (18in) square of tapestry canvas, 10 holes to
  2.5cm (1in)
Appletons tapestry wools (yarns) as follows:
  984 × 10 skeins,
  127 × 7 skeins,
  226 × 6 skeins,
  224 × 4 skeins,
  221 × 1 skein
  (You will need extra wool (yarn) to make the cord
  and tassels)
Size 24 tapestry needle
35cm (14in) square cushion pad
45cm (18in) square of toning cotton velvet or
  furnishing fabric for backing cushion
Tapestry frame or carpet tape

❶ Start the needlepoint by binding the edge of the canvas with tape, or mounting it on to a frame.

❷ Begin by stitching the dark coloured, left side of the diamond shapes. This will help you to accurately plot the position of the stripes in the trellis which should be worked next. The whole design is worked in half cross or tent stitch. Then fill in the remaining three colours of the diamond shapes and lastly the background.

❸ Stretch the needlepoint as described in Stretching (see page 41), ready to make it up into the cushion cover.

❹ Lay the piece of velvet or backing fabric on top of your needlepoint, with right sides together. Pin and tack (baste) all round, along the edge of the needlepoint. Machine stitch, leaving a 30cm (12in) gap in one side for turning. Trim the excess canvas and backing fabric diagonally across at the corners and 2.5cm (1in) away from the seam, all round. Turn right side out and insert the cushion pad. Pin the opening together, folding in the raw edges and then hand stitch to neaten.

❺ To finish the cushion in style, make up a 150cm (60in) length of twisted cord using three of the wool colours. You will need 3 strands of each colour. Hand stitch this all round the cushion, tucking the loose ends into the gap where you inserted the cushion pad. Sew the cord in place firmly but do not stretch it as you stitch or it will not lie flat. Make four, two-colour tassels using 2.5cm (1in) diameter cotton balls as the base and cutting the tassel strands to about 6cm (2.5in) long. Full instructions for the cord and tassels are on pages 96-9.

Choose rich terracotta shades for a subtly
warm look, just right amongst typical
Victorian furnishings.

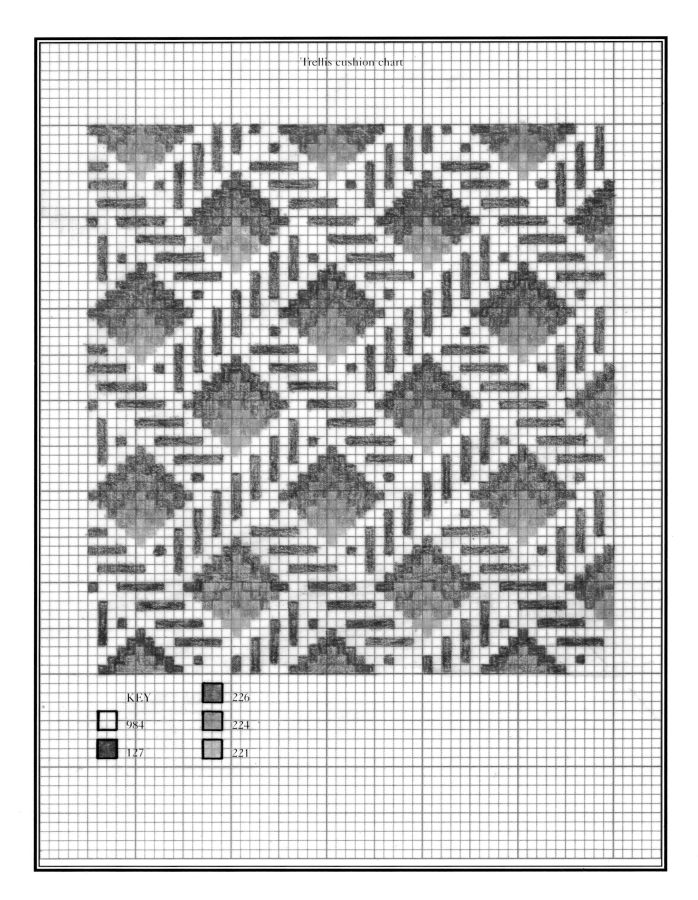

KEY

984

127

226

224

221

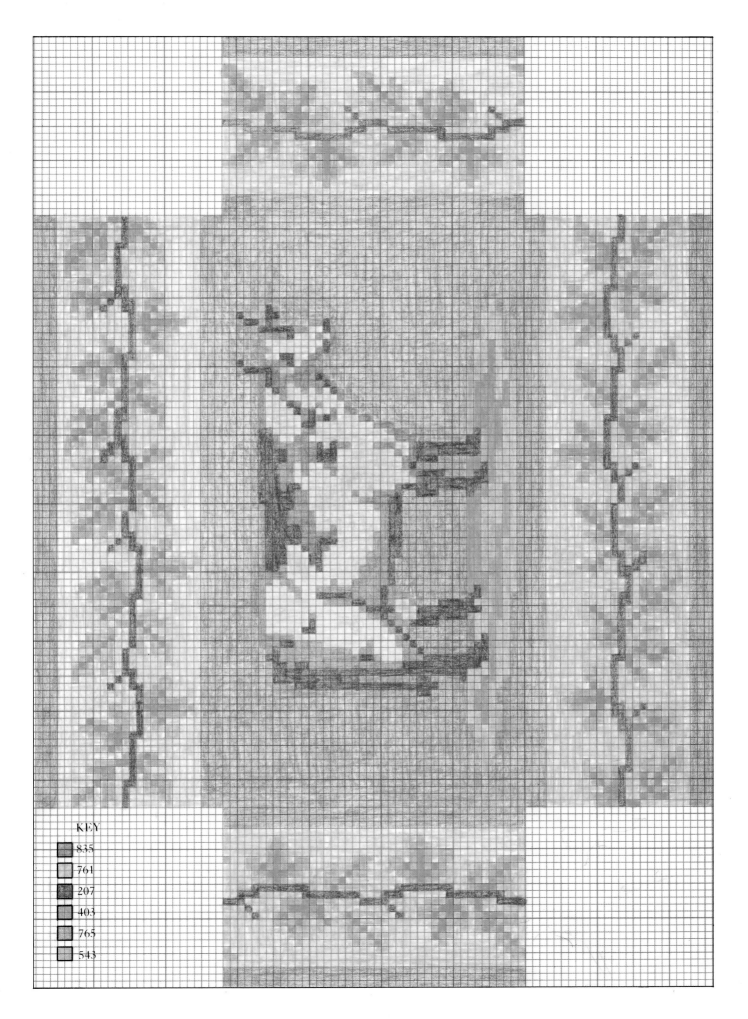

KEY
835
761
207
403
765
543

Country Cow Doorstop

This needlepoint doorstop is an interesting but not too demanding design for a beginner and ideal to make as a gift. To give the necessary weight to hold a door open, the finished needlepoint is wrapped round a standard house brick and stitched in place.

50 × 40cm (18 × 15in) double-thread tapestry
* canvas, 10 holes to 2.5cm (1in)*
Appletons tapestry wools (yarns) as follows:
* 835 × 5 skeins*
* 761 × 4 skeins*
* 207 × 2 skeins*
* 403 × 2 skeins*
* 765 × 1 skein*
* 543 × 1 skein*
Size 24 tapestry needle
Tapestry frame or carpet tape
A standard house brick
Darning needle
Linen carpet thread
Toning felt to cover the base
PVA glue or clear household adhesive

❶ Begin by binding the edges of the canvas with tape, or mounting it on to a frame. The whole design is worked in half cross or tent stitch.

❷ Mark the five rectangular areas of the chart (see page 53) centrally on to the canvas with tacking (basting) stitches. This may seem rather time-consuming, but it will save a great deal of counting later on and ensure that the needlepoint will fit the brick accurately.

❸ Stitch the central area of the chart first, working the cow, then the grass and then the background. Continue with the background colour on to the four side panels and then stitch the decorative leafy borders.

❹ Stretch the finished needlepoint as described in Stretching (see page 41) and use a set square and ruler to ensure it is accurate. Working on the reverse of the needlepoint, fold the side panels down and stitch the canvas layers together along the edge of the needlepoint. Use a strong darning needle with the linen carpet thread and backstitch the seam securely. Make a seam at each corner and then trim away the triangles of canvas close to the stitching.

❺ Slip the needlepoint over the brick, with the hollow part of the brick on the underside. Fold the remaining canvas neatly on to the base and oversew. If it seems rather lumpy, trim away any excess folds of canvas. Cut the felt to fit the base of the brick and glue it in place to neaten.

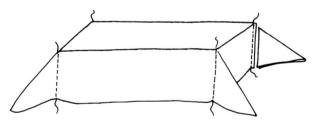

Stitching corners of doorstop

❻ If the surface of the brick seems rather scratchy, first cover it with a layer of thin calico or sheeting to protect the back of the canvas and stop it wearing through.

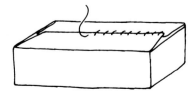

Oversewing base of doorstop

Needlecase

The original Victorian pieces shown on the previous page include several samplers, which are most frequently associated with cross stitch. However, small items such as this needlecase were often described in Victorian ladies' magazines as the perfect gift or keepsake. This delightful design is only two or three evenings' work.

Cross stitch is one of the simplest stitches to master. One of the few rules is that the top half of the stitch should always lie in the same direction all over the piece of work. This helps to keep it neat and allows your eye to see past the stitches to the pattern they have created.

It is nearly always worked on an evenweave fabric, which keeps the stitches a uniform size and shape. There is a fabric especially woven for cross stitch, called Aida, which consists of a grid of tiny woven blocks interspersed with holes. This makes the counting of the pattern very easy, particularly for a beginner. Aida is available in various sizes and colours and is an attractive and easy fabric to use.

The background of a cross stitch design is usually left unstitched, so that once you have embroidered the design, the piece is ready to be made up into the finished article. Before you make it up, press the embroidery carefully. Lay it face down on a piece of clean cotton fabric over a thick towel. Lay another piece of cotton on top and press gently with a steam iron. This method raises the texture of the stitches.

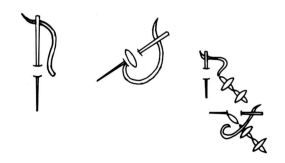

Cross stitch

30 × 18cm (12 × 7in) piece of white Aida evenweave fabric 11-gauge
DMC stranded embroidery cottons (floss):
  1 skein each of 3770, 761, 310, 3364, 899, 809, 775, 3362, 211, 209
Crewel embroidery needle
23cm (9in) square each of white and green felt
1m (1yd) narrow pink taffeta ribbon
PVA glue and spreader
A piece of stiff white card the same size as the evenweave fabric
Pinking shears

---

❶ Cut the embroidery cotton (floss) into 50cm (20in) lengths to avoid tangling. Then divide each piece in half and sew with three strands at a time.

❷ Following the chart and the key (page 60), embroider the flower wreath centrally, near one end of the fabric. Begin by stitching one whole flower and then work your way around the wreath. If the needlecase is a gift for someone you could embroider their initial in the centre. The letter I used is from the sampler but you may need to adapt the design slightly to fit in some of the larger letters.

❸ When you have finished the embroidery, press it as described. Trace off the inner dotted line for the shape of the needlecase. Cut out two of these shapes in stiff white card.

❹ Lay the embroidery on to the work surface,

right side down and place one card shape on top, so that the cross stitch design is central. Hold the fabric in place with pins pushed into the edge of the card. Lay the other card shape above the first one with the straight edges parallel and about 6mm (¼in) apart. Pin as before.

When the placing is correct, trim the excess fabric round the curved edges of the card leaving about 2.5cm (1in) of fabric showing all round. Snip into this excess fabric, almost up to the card, then fold the fabric pieces over and glue them to the back of the card shapes.

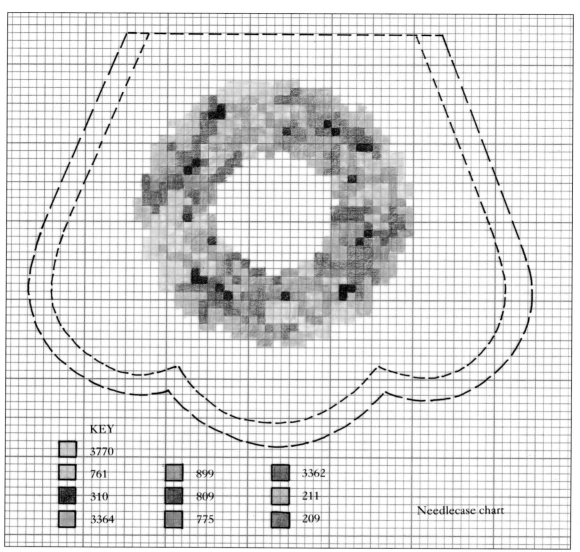

KEY

▢	3770						
▢	761	▨	899		▨	3362	
■	310	▨	809		▢	211	
▨	3364	▨	775		▨	209	

Needlecase chart

Sampler chart

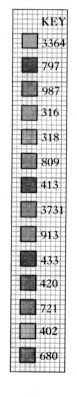

KEY

▢	3364
■	797
▨	987
▨	316
▨	318
▨	809
▨	413
▨	3731
▢	913
■	433
▨	420
▨	721
▢	402
■	680

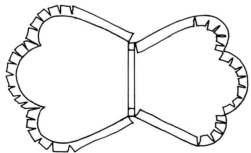

Snipping and folding over edges of needlecase

❺ Spread glue carefully over the whole of the back of the card pieces and lay on the piece of white felt to cover it completely. Press firmly all over and leave for the glue to dry. When it is ready, use sharp scissors to trim away the excess felt, level with the card.

❻ Trace off the outer dotted line from the pattern, fold the green felt square in half and pin the pattern on to it, so that the straight edge goes along the fold of the felt. Cut out the shape with pinking shears. Open out the needlecase and spread a line of glue along the inside fold. Lay the green felt inside and close the case. Leave the glue to set.

❼ Glue a piece of the ribbon along the inside fold leaving a loop on the outside of the needlecase. Tie two tiny bows and glue them to the outside of the case at each side. Tie another bow at the top of the loop and glue the ribbon ends to the back of the bow to make a half rosette.

60

Sampler

This typical mid-nineteenth century sampler shows a whole alphabet, both upper and lower case, and a wonderful library of borders and motifs that can be used on many different decorative items. The stitched area of the finished sampler measures approximately 35 × 24.5cm (13¾ × 9½in).

50cm (18in) of cream-coloured Aida evenweave
fabric 14-gauge
DMC stranded embroidery cottons (floss):
5 skeins each of 3364, 797, 987, 316, 318
3 skeins each of 809, 413, 3731, 913, 433, 420
2 skeins each of 721, 402, 680
Crewel embroidery needle
Graph paper
A frame to fit the finished sampler
Thick white card to fit your frame
Carpet thread and a large needle

---

❶ Start by making a line of tacking (basting) stitches vertically and horizontally across the fabric, to mark the centre. This will help you to position the design correctly.

❷ Following the chart and key (page 61), work the sampler in cross stitch. Divide the embroidery cotton (floss) and use three strands at a time. Use thread about 50cm (20in) long to avoid tangling as you sew. Each square on the chart equals one block of threads on the fabric.

❸ Working from the top downwards, stitch the alphabet and numbers first, then the rows of border patterns and the motifs.

❹ Using the letters and numbers on the chart, draw your chosen name and date on to the graph paper to fit into the given space. Fold this pattern in half to find the centre and then match this up with the central tacking (basting) line on the sampler. Stitch the name and date in place.

❺ Stitch the border last, in case you want to make any adjustments to the final shape to allow you to add more names or an actual birthday, rather than just the year you are commemorating.

❻ When the sampler is finished, press the embroidery as described. Place it over the piece of thick card, right side up and position it centrally, leaving equal amounts at the top and sides and a little more space at the bottom. Hold it in position with pins pushed into the edge of

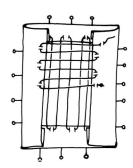

Lacing the back of the sampler

the card. Turn the card over and fold the surplus fabric to the back. Using the carpet thread and a large needle, lace the raw edges together, top to bottom and side to side, making sure that the weave of the fabric remains straight. Remove the pins and fix the sampler into your chosen frame.

Make the sampler look authentic by adding Victorian details such as your grandmother's name and date of birth.

Glasses Case

❦

This classical border pattern makes a simple but effective design for an elegant glasses case. The edges are piped in a toning colour and the sides are stiffened to protect the glasses.

30cm (12in) piece of 36-count cream linen
DMC stranded embroidery cottons (floss):
 1 skein each of 315 and 316
Crewel embroidery needle
Scraps of pink lawn for piping
51cm (20in) fine cord for piping
22 × 15cm (8½ × 6in) piece of thick, iron-on Vilene
 interfacing
Matching threads

---

❶ Cut out a 25 × 12.5cm (10 × 5in) piece of linen. Following the chart and key, embroider the cross stitch design centrally on to the piece of linen. Each square on the chart represents a block of 4 threads on the fabric.

❷ Cut the embroidery cotton (floss) into 50cm (20in) lengths to avoid tangling. Then divide each piece in half and sew with three strands at a time.

❸ Stitch the lighter colour first, to form the main part of the pattern, then stitch the remaining areas in the darker shade. Repeat this on a similar-sized piece of linen for the back of the case. Press both pieces of embroidery when finished.

❹ Trace off the rectangle shape from around the stitch chart. Use this to cut out two pieces of the Vilene interfacing. Following the maker's instructions, iron these centrally on to the back of each piece of embroidery.

❺ Using the toning lawn fabric, cut some 2.5cm (1in) wide bias strips. Join these to make a piece about 51cm (20in) long. Wrap this around the

Covering cord with bias strips

cord and tack (baste) in place, with the right side of the fabric outside, to make piping for the front and back of the case. Cut the length of piping in half and lay it on the right side of the embroidered pieces, with the tacking (basting) line on

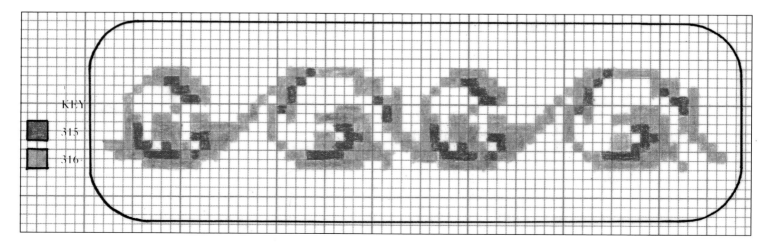

KEY

315
316

This repeating scroll pattern is very versatile and could be used as an attractive border for samplers and cushions.

the piping following the edge of the interfacing. Snip into the edge of the piping fabric to help it lie smoothly round the curved corners. Pin and stitch the piping round the edge, tucking in the raw ends neatly where they meet.

❻ Trim the linen level with the raw edge of the piping cord fabric. Use this as a guide to cut out two more pieces of linen to line each embroidered piece. Press under the edges on the lining pieces and hand stitch them in place to enclose all the raw edges.

❼ To make the gusset, cut out two pieces of the linen 20.5 × 2.5cm (8 × 1in). Fold them in half

across the width. Tuck in the long raw edges and press, to make the gusset pieces about 13mm (½in) wide. Stitch down each long side. Hand stitch each gusset piece in place to join the front and back pieces of the glasses case. Place the gusset fold near the top of the case and tuck the raw ends inside where they meet underneath.

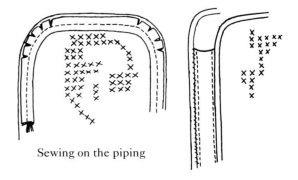

Sewing on the piping

Sewing the gusset
in place

Bookmark

A pretty bookmark is a perfect first project if you are a beginner at cross stitch. It is an attractive gift for men and women and would be quick to make for bazaars and country fairs.

30 × 15cm (12 × 6in) piece of green Aida evenweave
fabric 14-gauge
DMC stranded embroidery cottons (floss):
1 skein each of 413, 402, 721, 420, 3363, 433
22.5 × 4.5cm (8¾ × 1¾in) piece of stiff card
Crewel needle
Sewing needle and green thread
PVA glue

❶ Cut the embroidery cotton (floss) into 50cm (20in) lengths to avoid tangling. Then divide each piece in half and sew with three strands at a time.

❷ Following the chart and the key, embroider the design centrally on to the fabric. Begin with the green branched part of the design and then stitch the straight grey borders. Next work the stylized floral areas. When you have finished the embroidery, press the back of the fabric as described.

❸ Lay the embroidery down on the work surface, wrong side uppermost, and place the card exactly over the embroidered area. Hold the fabric in place, with pins pushed into the edge of the card. Fold the remaining fabric round the card turning the long raw edge under, and glue in place to the card.

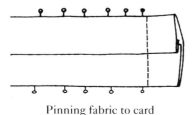

Pinning fabric to card

❹ Stitch through the fabric at the ends of the card to neaten. Trim the excess fabric 2.5cm (1in) from the card ends and, using a needle, fray most of the fabric ends to make fringes.

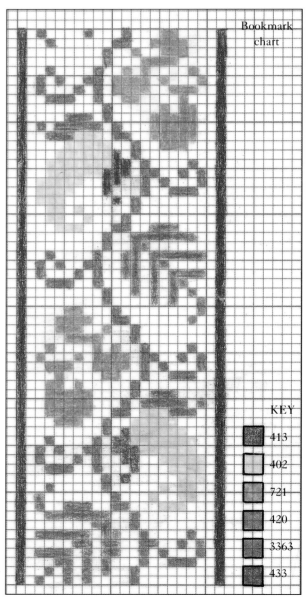

Bookmark chart

KEY
	413
	402
	721
	420
	3363
	433

Experiment with different coloured
fabrics and embroidery cottons to make several
bookmarks in a variety of colourways.

Beadwork

Beaded Pendant Earrings

Beads were used by the million in Victorian times to decorate all sorts of needlework, garments, footstools, purses and fringes as shown in the selection of original Victorian pieces on the previous page. To begin with, beads were available in a limited range of colours that were only suitable for very simple patterns and backgrounds. The variety of colours was much improved with the import of beads from Venice and Germany to create the vibrant hued patterns, some of which still exist in good condition today. As with many Victorian crafts, beadwork requires patience in greater quantity than skill, although using the correct tools and methods is a great help. Beads were often stitched in with Berlin woolwork to highlight certain areas and you can do this with the needlepoint designs in this book if you choose beads that are the same size as the canvas mesh.

These pretty pendant earrings are reminiscent of Victorian style and are still in fashion today. They are easy and quite quick to make and you can choose a selection of tiny beads to match your outfit perfectly.

Jewellery findings or ear wires
Glass bugle beads
Small round glass beads (seed beads)
Beading needle
Nylon beading thread

BASIC EARRING

❶ Using the nylon thread in a beading needle, begin the earring with the central row of long bugle beads. Thread on two beads and then go back up through the first one and back down through the second, so that they lie next to each other.

❷ Thread on the next bead and go back through the second and up through the third again. Continue in this way until you have joined nine

Threading two bugle beads together

Adding a third bead

beads. The thread should come out at the top of the last bead.

❸ Thread on a round bead, go under the first loop of thread on top of the bugle beads and back through the round bead, so that it stands up. Thread on another round bead, go under the next loop of thread and back up through the

Threading on the round beads

You can make all kinds of variations on this earring design using different amounts and colours of beads. Always start with an uneven numbered row of bugle beads.

---

same bead. Continue working like this to the end of the row (8 beads).

❹ Turn the earring over and work along the top in the same way. The second row will have 7 beads and each subsequent row will have one bead less, gradually coming to a point at the top of the earring with a single bead.

❺ Now thread on 6 round beads, pass the needle through the loop of the ear wire and back through the top bead. Thread down through the diagonal edge of the earring and through to the bottom of the first bugle bead.

❻ Now make the beaded fringe for the earring.

Thread on 7 beads of your choice then turn and go back up through the second-to-last bead, up through the bugle bead and down through the next bugle bead. Continue the fringe, making each strand a little longer, until you reach the longest one in the centre. Finish by threading up through the sloping edge of the earring and round the earring loop. Tie off the thread neatly and trim the end.

Taking the loop through the earring wire

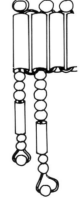

Working the fringe

Beaded Bottles

This method of beadwork is known as bead mosaic work. It was very popular in the mid-nineteenth century, being used to make lampshades, napkin rings and even fancy baskets. It consists of joining rows of beads, without the use of any backing material, so that a flat bead 'fabric' is constructed and the beading fits exactly as in these beaded bottles. The same method was used to adorn the handles of parasols, knives and walking canes in Victorian times.

A variety of different small, round beads (seed beads)
Beading needle
Nylon beading thread
Bottles or handles to decorate

❶ Using the nylon thread in the beading needle, thread on the first circle of beads so that they fit exactly round the base of the bottle. This should be an even number. Push the needle through the line of beads, to join it into a circle, so that the thread goes round the bottle twice. Fasten it to the beginning of the thread. This makes a secure foundation row. Hold it in place round the base of the bottle.

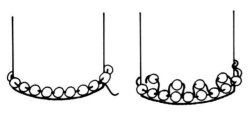

Working the foundation row   Threading on a second row of beads

❷ For the next row, thread on one bead at a time. In between each new bead, go down to the first row and thread through every other foundation bead before coming up to thread on a new one. This means that the second and sub-

sequent rows use half the number of beads as in the foundation row.

❸ Repeat the beading up the bottle as far as you wish to go. It is advisable to work the first two or three rows in a single colour until you master the technique. Later it is easy to work in simple patterns and stripes.

❹ To finish off the top edge, make a decorative border. To do this, start the row as usual with a new bead, then instead of going into the lower row, thread on two more beads. Take the needle back through the second bead and then

Working the top row

thread on a fourth. Now pass the needle through the next-but-one bead on the lower row. Continue in this way all around to form the edging. If the lid is suitable, work beading round this in the same way.

Richly coloured beading turns a simple bottle into a thing of beauty, worthy of a place on the most elegant dressing table.

Beaded Lampshade

In Victorian times beaded fringes were a feature of nearly every drawing room or parlour. Lampshades of all descriptions were adorned with them, particularly the attractive tiffany-shaped ones as featured here.

Small tiffany lampshade
Small round beads in red, petrol blue, clear gold and clear mauve
Larger round beads in clear pale yellow
Beading needle
Nylon beading thread
White cotton tape to bind frame
Braid to go round edge of lampshade

❶ Carefully remove any braid at the base of the shade. This will need to be replaced once the fringe has been stitched in place. If you wish to use a lampshade frame you will need to bind the frame and make a simple cover before you start the fringe.

❷ Each string of beads is the same length for this fringe; the scalloped effect comes from the scalloped edge to the frame. If your shade has a straight edge, you can still achieve this scalloped effect by adding extra beads and lengthening and shortening the strands gradually, to form the scallops.

❸ Start by threading your beading needle with a length of the nylon thread. Tie a knot in the end and thread on the 40 beads following the

pattern. Start from the top and when you reach the end, turn and push the needle back through the large bead and up to the top of the string again. The best way to work with the tiny beads is to tip a few of each colour into separate saucers and pick them up with the point of the needle.

❹ Pull both ends of the thread until they are level and snip off the knot. Thread both ends into a sewing needle and firmly oversew the string of beads to the outside edge of the lampshade.

❺ Continue in this way, sewing on each string as soon as it is threaded. Stitch the strings of beads a little way apart, allowing for the larger beads at the ends to hang straight. Finish the shade by gluing on a piece of toning braid to cover all the stitching.

Chart for order of beads

KEY

●   Petrol blue

○   Clear mauve

●   Red

○   Clear gold

◯   Clear pale yellow

Threading on the
large end bead

A beaded fringe makes the perfect shade to go with a Victorian wall light, whether antique or reproduction.

Lacy Beaded Covers

The Victorians loved their things to be practical as well as pretty – these enchanting beaded covers are typical of the period. Jugs and basins of food were left in the larder or on a tea table covered in this way, to keep out dust and insects. You can still buy these covers but the ones shown here can be made very easily from scraps of cotton lace with a simple crocheted edging to attach the beads.

Scraps of cotton lace curtaining
Glass beads with large holes
2.50mm (No 12) crochet hook
Twilleys Southern Comfort crochet cotton

❶ Cut the lace into circles, keeping any large motif in the centre. The small cover is 20cm

(8in) diameter and the large one is 28cm (11in) diameter.

❷ For the small cover, thread about 40 large blue beads on to the crochet cotton before you begin. Work double crochet into the edge of the lace circle to stop it from fraying.

Then work as follows: 1dc into 1st ch, * 8ch, miss 2ch, 1dc into next ch *. Repeat from * to * moving one bead into position on to each 8ch loop as you work, and ending with ss into first dc. Fasten off.

❸ For the large cover, thread on about 40 large green beads for the outer edge and about 76 mixed small blue, green and mauve beads for the first two rows of the fringe. Then work as follows:

1st round: 1dc into 1st ch * 6ch, miss 4ch, 1dc into next ch *. Repeat from * to * moving one small bead on to each 6ch loop as you work. **2nd round:** ss to centre of first 6ch loop, * 8ch, 1dc into next loop *. Repeat from * to * moving the beads into place as before. **3rd round:** ss to centre of first 8ch loop, * 12ch, 1dc into next loop *. Repeat from * to * moving the large green beads into place as before and ending with ss into first dc. Fasten off.

Use these delightful lacy covers for tea in the garden to stop unwanted insects invading your food.

A Merry Christmas
and a bright New Year.

May the
New Year
be to You one of
Peace and Gladness

Papercraft

Paper Lace Pictures and Box

❦

Paper doilies and pierced decorations make charming pictures, cards and mounts as shown in the selection of Victorian scraps and doilies on the previous page. We can achieve similar results with ready-cut paper mats.

A selection of white paper doilies in different shapes and sizes
PVA glue and a spreader or spray glue
Small sharp scissors
Coloured card
Suitable pictures cut from greetings cards, magazines or paper scraps
Craft knife and cutting board

❶ Start by selecting a favourite picture or motif. Then decide whether the subject would look better with the lace decoration as an under or an over mount. An under mount is best when the picture can be cut out from its background and has an attractive and detailed outline.

Sometimes a complete doily will work well as an under mount with very few additions. More often than not, you will need to trim off certain areas of the doily and add pieces here and there to the edge to make just the right shape. The best way to work is to experiment with lots of different pieces, laying out your design on to a coloured background.

❷ When you are happy with the design, spread or spray glue on to the reverse of the doily and then lay it in place on the coloured card. Lay a piece of clean paper on top and press gently to attach the doily all over. Do not press too hard or you will flatten some of the embossing and spoil the design.

❸ Next cut out the picture following the outline and carefully preserving all the detail. Glue the back of the picture and place it centrally on to the paper lace.

❹ For an over mount, lay your chosen picture on to a large piece of coloured card and experiment by cutting the plain centre shapes out of several doilies. Lay them on top of the picture to find the best one, trimming off any pieces that overlap too much. Glue the picture in place first and then the lacy mount. Lastly cut the card out to leave a margin round the edge.

❺ Another way of using doilies is to carefully cut out small scrolls, flowers and motifs from different doilies. Glue your print on to white or pale coloured card and then build up an outer frame from the pieces of doily. Work so that the design is symmetrical and the pieces are evenly spaced. This is also an excellent way to decorate the edge of a paper-covered photo frame.

❻ The oval wooden box in the picture has also been decorated with doilies. Edging strips from a big rectangular doily have been glued round the sides and the top is completely covered with lacy paper from the centre of another large doily. When making a box the lacy paper needs to be glued on much more firmly than for a picture mount. Use PVA glue for this project, spreading it very thoroughly over the back of the paper. A selection of cut out reproduction Victorian scraps completes the effect. A thin coat of clear varnish is advisable to protect the surface of your box.

A charming collection of paper lace decorations.

Tartan Ware

The Victorian fascination for tartan patterns developed as a result of Queen Victoria's love affair with Scotland. Soon, souvenirs and all manner of small household and needlework items were made in wood or papier mâché and then decorated with different tartan designs. To start with, these designs were painstakingly painted on to the surfaces but later, a machine for printing tartan paper was invented. The paper was glued in place and then varnished.

This set of tartan desk accessories (see overleaf) has been made as a modern alternative to the increasingly scarce original Victorian pieces. I have used basically the same method of gluing and varnishing the paper in place, but omitted the black lines which were often used to disguise the joins. Instead of the modern glue/varnish I have used, you could give these pieces an antique-look crackle finish, using the technique described on page 106.

Good quality tartan wrapping paper
Mod Podge glue/varnish
Tartan patterned taffeta ribbon
Brushes
Scissors and craft knife
Wooden box
Wooden letter rack
Cardboard cocoa pot
Tiny wooden frames
Large empty sticky tape reels (cardboard)
Small ball of string
Thick and thin card

PHOTO FRAMES

❶ Remove all the backing card and glass from the frame. Using scrap paper, make a template of each side of the frame ready to cut out the tartan paper. Lay the paper over one side of the frame, hold it in place and carefully cut along both mitres with a craft knife. Fold the edges of

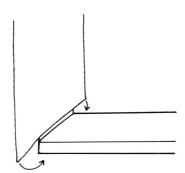

Making template for frame

Tartan ware photo frames.

the paper round the frame and trim off at the back. Make sure this is accurate. For a rectangular frame, make another template for the longer or shorter side.

❷ Lay these templates on to the back of the tartan paper and draw round them. Cut out and try each piece in position on the frame. Trim if necessary and then spread the back with glue. Press each piece in place pushing out any air bubbles. Fold the extra paper round to the back of the frame to neaten.

❸ When the glue is dry, brush on several more coats of Mod Podge to act as a varnish, leaving it to dry between coats. Make a tiny bow from the tartan ribbon and paint it with several coats of Mod Podge to stiffen it. When it is dry, glue it centrally to the top of the frame.

LETTER RACK

❶ If the pieces of your letter rack are glued together, work as for the frames, using scrap paper to make templates for each surface. Cut them out accurately in tartan paper and glue them in place to leave a narrow margin of wood showing around the edge. Varnish as before.

❷ If your letter rack comes to pieces or is a DIY kit, you can cover each piece with the tartan paper, trim it flush with the edge and then assemble it into the letter rack. Varnish it when complete.

BLOTTER

❶ Cut out a piece of thick card 33 × 25cm (13 × 10in) and another piece slightly smaller. Cut out four 7.5cm (3in) wide strips of tartan paper and glue these in place over the edges of the larger card piece.

❷ On thin card, draw out four right-angled triangles with their sides measuring 8cm (3¼in). Cut them out using a craft knife. Cut out tartan paper triangles about 1.5cm (¾in) larger than the card triangles. Spread glue on to the back of the paper and place the card pieces on centrally. Fold the excess paper to the back of the card on the long side only. Line each triangle up with the corners of the large rectangle and glue the remaining excess paper on the sides of the triangle, to the back of the thick card.

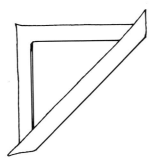

Folding paper round card triangle

❸ Glue the smaller piece of card to the back of the blotter to cover the folded over edges of the paper. Varnish over the tartan paper with several coats of Mod Podge. To complete, tuck blotting paper under the corner pieces.

STORAGE BOX

❶ Whatever the size or shape of your chosen box, the method for covering it will be the same. Concentrate on the outside surfaces first, folding the excess paper to the inside and then neaten the interior of the box to complete.

❷ First cut a piece of paper that will go round the lower half of the box, overlapping slightly at the back and with excess paper at the top and bottom. Glue this in place, snipping the excess paper at the corners so that it will fold over the edges of the box neatly.

❸ Cut an oversized piece of paper for the top of the box lid. Glue it in place, snipping and folding over the excess paper as before. Cut a strip of paper for the sides of the lid. Glue it in place so that the edge is flush with the top of the lid. Fold the lower edge to the inside. Lastly neaten the box base with a slightly smaller square of paper or felt to protect the furniture. Varnish

the outside of the box and leave it to dry.

❹ Finish the inside of the box by covering thin pieces of card, cut slightly smaller than the sides, with contrasting paper or fabric and gluing them in place.

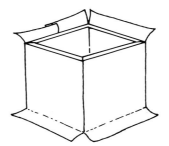

Gluing paper around box

STRING HOLDER

❶ Save two or three large inner rings from sticky tape and glue them on top of each other to make a short tube. Cut two circles of thin card to fit the top and base of the tube. Cover the circles with a larger piece of tartan paper. Make a small hole in the centre of one circle for the top of the string holder. Glue this circle on top of the tubes, snipping the edge of the surplus paper and gluing it to the sides of the holder.

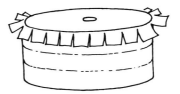

Gluing circle on to tubes

❷ Turn the whole thing over and put the ball of string inside, threading the end of it through the hole. Now glue on the base circle in the same way as the top. Cut a strip of the tartan paper to fit round the sides of the holder and glue it in place. Protect with two or three coats of varnish.

Turn a simple side table into a writing area with this smart collection of tartan desk accessories.

PENCIL HOLDER AND PENCILS

Tartan pencil holder and string box.

❶ Simply remove the lid from the cocoa pot and glue on a strip of tartan paper round the outside of the pot. Trim the paper so that you leave the top and bottom edge of the pot showing. Varnish and then make a tartan bow as for the frames.

❷ Cover the pencils in the same way, with the tartan paper running diagonally round the pencil. Protect with two or three coats of varnish.

Quilled Boxes and Pictures

Quilling, or paper filigree, was a popular ladies' pastime in Victorian times. Decorative pictures, tea caddies and even whole cabinets were covered with these tiny spirals of paper, making intricate patterns and floral representations. Sometimes the paper rolls were coloured or even gilded to resemble fine gold filigree work.

Thin white cartridge paper
Sharp craft knife
Cutting board
Long metal ruler
Scissors
Quilling tool, cocktail stick, narrow dowelling or a
*   knitting needle for rolling the paper strips*
Tweezers
PVA glue and small brush
Silver or gold spray paint
Stiff card for mounting
Tiny pill boxes with recessed lids
Round picture frame about 12cm (4¾in) internal
*   diameter, to fit the pattern*

❶ Using the craft knife and cutting board, cut the paper into long thin strips about 3mm (⅛in) wide. These should be accurately cut, so that the surface of the quilling is level when the design is complete.

❷ The next stage is rolling the paper into different shaped scrolls. The variation in shape is determined by the length of the paper strip and the method of gluing and pinching the coil before they are arranged into the design. Try experimenting with a few different shapes until you get the feel of it.

❸ Slot the end of the paper strip into the slit in the top of the quilling tool and then wind the paper round firmly, keeping it level. If you glue the end in place now and then remove the

Closed coil

paper from the tool, you will have a closed coil that will remain in this shape. These are very useful for filling in areas and making borders. If, however, you remove the paper before gluing, it will unroll slightly and the layers will open out. Glue the end in place at this stage and you have a simple open coil. This is the most usual method for quilling, enabling you to pinch and shape the coil as follows:

TEAR DROP
Pinch an open coil at one side, after gluing.

Tear drop

PETAL
Make as for the tear drop but curl the pinched end round.

Petal

EYE

Pinch the coil at both sides simultaneously.

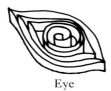

Eye

LEAF

Pinch both sides as for the eye and curl round in opposite directions.

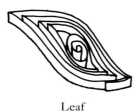

Leaf

HALF MOON

Press the coil gently round the tool handle and pinch the ends.

Half moon

TRIANGLE

Fold to make the half moon but pinch the top as well.

Triangle

RECTANGLE OR SQUARE

Pinch two opposite corners as for the eye then pinch two more to form either a square or rectangle.

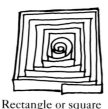

Rectangle or square

❹ When you have mastered all these shapes, make up a few of each and start to lay them out to form patterns. To make regular designs you will need to keep constant the length of the strip you are using, so that all the pieces in that motif remain the same size and shape.

PILL BOXES

❶ The tiny pill boxes are probably the best projects to start with as they are quite simple and quick to complete and the outer rim of the lid helps to hold the scrolls in place as you design your pattern.

❷ Make up several different shapes and arrange them on the lid to form an attractive design. When you are happy with the design, lift each piece with tweezers and paint a little glue on the base of the coil. Replace it at once and glue the next coil. Continue in this way over the whole area. Sometimes it helps to paint a small amount of glue on the sides of the coils as well, to adhere them to the ones touching. But be sparing with the glue so that it does not show, thus spoiling the finished effect.

❸ When the glue has dried, you can colour the whole box with silver or gold spray paint. Stand the open box inside an empty cardboard grocery carton, to protect the surrounding area from paint. Spray gently, following the maker's instructions, aiming for several light coatings so that the design does not fill in. Turn the box base and lid round as they dry so that they are evenly covered.

❹ You can also spray the inside of the box or line it with scraps of paper or fine fabric. Finally, decorate the outside of the box with ribbon and a tiny bow if you wish.

Tiny pill boxes make beautiful little jewel cases for a single pair of earrings or a special ring. A white box would be a lovely keepsake for a bridesmaid's gift.

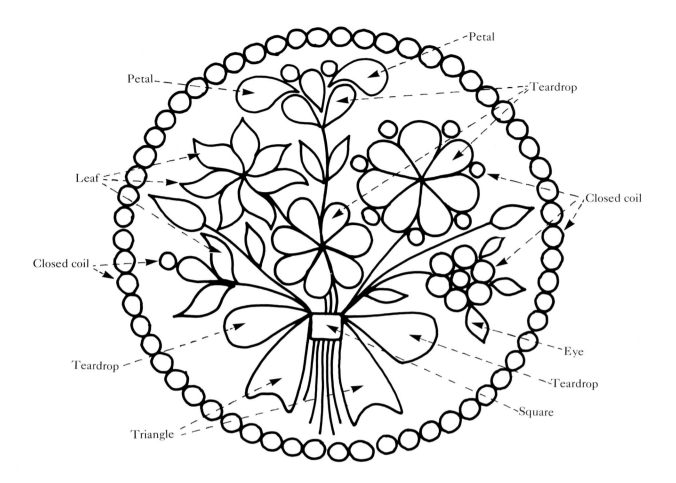

Petal

Petal

Teardrop

Leaf

Closed coil

Closed coil

Eye

Teardrop

Teardrop

Square

Triangle

Pattern for quilled picture

QUILLED PICTURE

❶ Using the glass from the frame as a guide, cut out a circle of white card to be the base for your design. Place the card in the frame and begin the picture by making lots of closed coils using 15cm (6in) long strips. Glue these to the card all round the inside edge of the frame to make a border.

❷ Now use the full-size pattern as a guide and make up the various coils as indicated. The stems are made from folded pieces of the paper strips curved into shape and trimmed to length. Arrange the pieces and glue them in place to complete the design. You can work with the card out of the frame at this stage if it is easier. Assemble the quilling design in the frame with the glass to protect it, if you wish.

With a little more expertise you can make this delicate filigree picture to decorate a small corner.

Papier Mâché

❧

Papier mâché was originally made to imitate the fashionable lacquer work that was imported from China in the eighteenth century. The Victorians were very keen on papier mâché as it was considerably cheaper and could be made at home by a talented crafts person. The designs I have created here are reminiscent of the art nouveau penwork designs that were so popular in the latter half of the century.

BASIC METHOD

Newspaper, preferably in two different colours
Ruler
PVA glue
Bristle brush
Vaseline
Small bowl to use as a mould
Card tube from kitchen roll
Gesso or canvas primer
Scissors
Fine grade sandpaper
Clear polyurethane varnish
Gold and black paint
Small water-colour brushes

---

❶ The basic method for this type of papier mâché is by laminating strips of newspaper, in layers, over a mould.

❷ Select the mould you are going to use and spread it liberally with Vaseline. Use either the outside or the inside surface, so that the papier mâché will come away easily when it is dry. Tear the newspaper into strips by pulling several layers at a time against a long ruler. Tear these into short pieces. Mix the PVA glue with a little water in an old dish, until it is the consistency of single cream (half-and-half). Brush the surface of your mould with some glue and then paste on some paper strips with the brush dipped in glue, so that you keep the surface sticky. Place the strips regularly and make an even layer all over. Make the second layer in the other colour of newspaper so that you can check that the mould is completely covered, and then do a third layer.

❸ At this stage it is best to leave the papier mâché to dry in a warm place for a few hours until the surface is touch dry. Repeat this process working three layers and letting them dry in between until you reach the desired thickness. You can test the thickness on soft papier mâché, by pushing in a pin as far as it will go and marking the place with your thumbnail as you pull it out. About ten or twelve layers is probably enough.

❹ Now leave the papier mâché to dry out completely. When it is really dry it will sound hard when you tap it. While it is drying you can gently ease it away from the mould with a blunt knife, to help release it later.

Drying times vary but it may take up to a week for it to get really hard. When it is ready, remove the mould and clean off any Vaseline. Trim any rough or uneven edges with scissors and apply the first coat of gesso with a brush. When this

---

Rich black and gold art nouveau designs are painted on to the finished papier mâché bangles, napkin ring and bowl.

has dried, rub it smooth with fine grade sandpaper and apply another coat. For a very fine surface, repeat this process several times.

❺ Once you have reached the required finish, paint the whole piece with one or two coats of black paint. Using a very fine paint brush and the gold paint, lightly indicate the pattern outline using the designs on this page as a guide. If you make a mistake quickly wipe it off before it dries. When the painting is complete, leave it to dry and then brush on a coat of varnish to give it a hard protective finish.

DECORATIVE BOWL

This was formed round the outside of a cereal dish. Radiate the strips of paper out from the centre, taking care to keep the finish as smooth as possible as you build up the layers. Let the papier mâché overlap the edge of the bowl and then trim this level just before you remove the mould. Finish as described.

ART NOUVEAU BANGLES

❶ Choose a fairly slim, straight-sided plastic bottle. Grease it with Vaseline, then paste 2.5cm (1in) strips of newspaper round it. Paste on the strips so that they are on top of each other and overlap the ends in a different place on each layer to avoid making lumps. Apply about six layers in this way to make the base for the bangle. You could make several bangles of different widths at the same time on one bottle.

❷ Leave the papier mâché to dry hard and then slip the bangles off the bottle. Trim the edges level with the scissors. Now paste on narrower strips of paper going in the opposite direction,

until the bangle is quite thick. You can build up the centre of the bangle to achieve a domed effect. Leave until hard and then sand, apply gesso, paint and varnish as described.

NAPKIN RING

Cut off a 2.5cm (1in) wide slice from a kitchen roll tube. Cover it with glue inside and out and paste on short strips of newspaper, as for the bangle. Finish as before.

Papier mâché designs

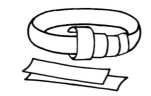

Making bangle with paper strips

94

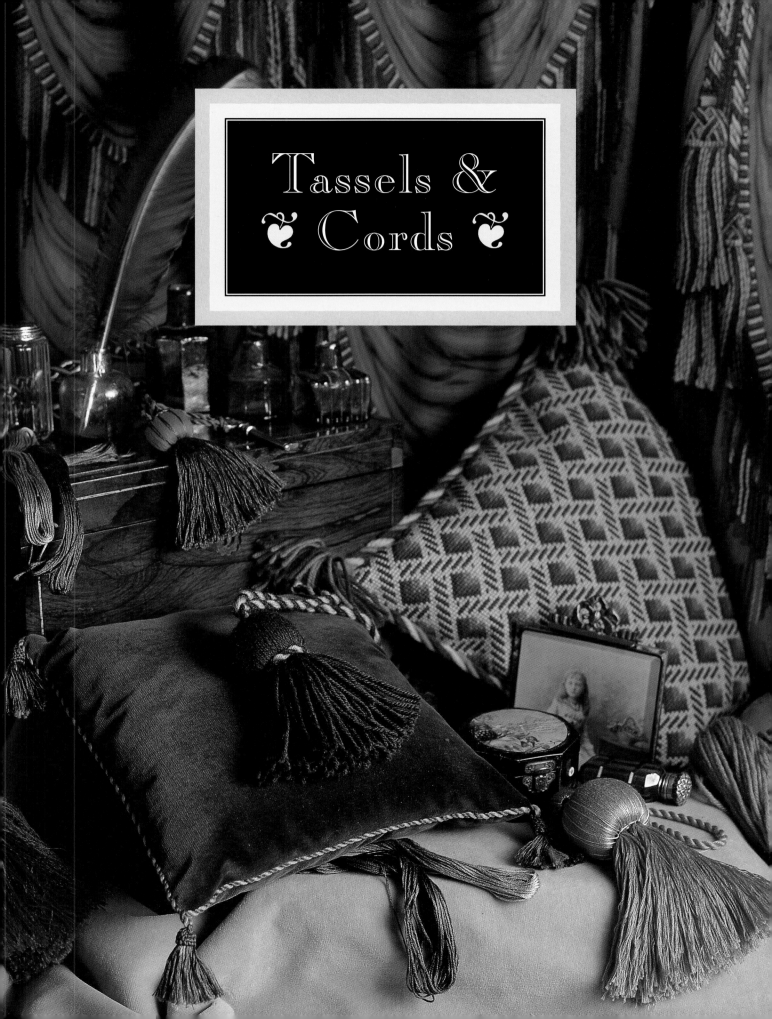

Tassels & Cords

Tassels

Tassels are most satisfying to make in all sorts of different shapes and sizes. You can make exactly the right tassel for each project and you may find that you enjoy making them so much that you want to take it up as a pastime in itself. A single beautiful tassel looks very handsome adorning a special key for a bureau or jewel box. There are several different methods for making tassels and I have featured the two most useful versions with a few variations. The proportions of any tassel should be approximately one third head and two thirds tail.

BASIC AND STITCHED-HEAD TASSEL

❶ Cut a piece of stiff card about 5cm (2in) wide and a little deeper than the length of the whole tassel. Wind the yarn round the card between twenty and forty times, depending on the thickness of your yarn and the size of the required tassel. (If you are making a set of tassels, keep count of the number of times you wind round the card so that all the tassels will be the same.) If you want the tail to include two or more colours, wind the different colours round the card together to disperse the colours evenly.

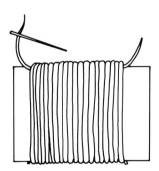

Winding wool around card

❷ Thread a tapestry needle with a long piece of the yarn and slip this under the wound yarn, next to the card. Do this several times and then tie the ends to hold all the strands together. You can also insert a twisted cord at this stage

for hanging up the finished tassel. Slip the yarn off the card.

❸ Push the needle down through the top of the tassel and bring it out about a third of the way down. Wind the yarn tightly round the tassel a few times to form the head. Knot securely and feed the ends back into the tassel. (You can stop at this stage for the basic tassel and go straight to step 6 to complete it.)

Tying top of tassel

❹ To enlarge the size of the head, you can pad it with cotton wool or synthetic wadding. Tear off small pieces and push them inside the head with a blunt needle. Stuff the head evenly, pulling the yarn round to hide the wadding.

❺ To complete the head, turn the tassel the other way up and work buttonhole stitch round and round. Start the first row of stitches by going into the strands round the tassel and then

Padding tassel head

work into the previous row, inserting the needle between each stitch. You can decrease the number of stitches as you reach the top by going between every other stitch. (You can decorate the tassel head with lines of stem stitch in contrasting coloured yarn as I did for the sewing casket tassel.)

Working buttonhole stitch

❻ Push the needle down through the tassel to finish off. Lastly cut the loops at the base of the tassel so that the ends are even.

Cutting tassel ends

BALL-BASED TASSEL

Use spun paper balls to form the smooth tassel heads in this version.

❶ Using the tip of your scissors, dig into the hole in the centre of the paper ball. Find the end and carefully pull out some of the paper from the inside, to enlarge the hole. The hole should be about half the size of the ball.

Enlarging hole in ball

❷ Thread a large needle with some of the chosen yarn. Make a loop knot in the end and pass the needle through the hole in the ball. Bring the yarn round and push the needle through the loop to secure. Pull the knot round to the inside of the ball and keep passing the needle through the hole to cover the ball with yarn. Aim for a single, even layer of yarn for a smooth finish. Don't pull the yarn too tightly or you will spoil the shape of the ball. You can add stripes of other colours or even metallic threads for variation.

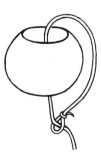

Tying wool to ball

❸ Make the tail by winding yarn round stiff card, as for the basic tassel. Slip a cord through the top of the yarn loops, tie and then remove from the card. Thread the cord through the hole in the tassel head and pull the tail up into the ball so that the top comes about half the way through.

Adding tassel tail

❺ Cut and trim the tail so that the strands are even. If you are using stranded embroidery cotton (floss) you can 'comb' the tail with scissor points to fluff out the fibres.

Top of tassel

❹ Thread a needle with some of the same yarn and make a few stitches to attach the tail firmly to the head. Use this yarn or metallic thread to work circles of buttonhole stitch to hide the hole in the tassel head if necessary.

This attractive tassel is worked in DMC stranded embroidery cotton. The top of the head is decorated with buttonhole stitch to fill in the hole neatly after the cord has been attached.

Cord

Twisted cord is really easy to make, with the help of one or two other people, depending on how many colours you are using. One minute it is a few strands of coloured yarn and the next, you have a beautifully even, twisted cord ready to enhance your best piece of work.

SINGLE COLOURED CORD

❶ To make a narrow, one colour cord, you will need another person and a piece of yarn about six times as long as the required length of the finished piece. (3m/3yd of yarn will make 50cm/18in of cord.) Fold the yarn in half and tie a knot in both ends.

❷ Each person holds a knot and twists the yarn in a clockwise direction. When it is tightly wound, hold the middle of the yarn with one hand and bring the two knots together; the strands will immediately twist round each other. Tie the two knots together and smooth down the length of cord until it becomes evenly twisted. Make thicker versions of this by using several lengths of yarn.

MULTICOLOURED CORD

❶ To make thicker, multicoloured cord, as shown on the needlepoint cushion on page 95, the method is slightly different. For three coloured cord, you will need three people and two or more pieces of yarn three times as long as the required length of the finished piece. (3m/3yd of each strand of yarn will make 1m/1yd of finished cord.)

❷ Hold all the strands of one colour together. Fold them in half and knot the free ends together. Repeat this with the other coloured yarns. Now give one knot to each person to hold and tie the three folded ends together in the middle. As before, twist in a clockwise direction until quite tight then bring the outer knots together whilst holding the central knot with the other hand. Tie the ends together and smooth down the cord until it is even.

❸ Before you cut the cord, you must secure it both sides of the cut, or it will come unravelled. To do this, wind a piece of yarn tightly round the cord and tie the ends securely. Repeat this process a short distance away and then cut the cord between the ties.

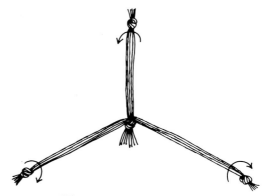

Winding three-coloured cord

❹ You can also use this method for finishing off the end of a piece of cord. Wind a piece of yarn round the cord near where you want the end, cut it and then untwist the cut ends and trim them into a simple tassel.

Binding cord

Découpage

Découpage

❦

Découpage is the art of cutting out pretty paper scraps and applying them, with glue and varnish, to many different surfaces to give the effect of a beautifully painted decoration.

This delightful craft was at its height in the mid-eighteenth century with the vogue for eastern design and lacquerwork; then the Victorian ladies took it up again in the next century, with renewed vigour. It was described as an amusing occupation for long evenings and required little artistic skill. It was an easy way of applying sentimental, amusing and beautiful decoration to a wide variety of items made from both metal and wood.

The secret of good découpage work is to make it look as though the design has been painted on to the surface. To achieve this effect, the paper shape needs to be cut out very accurately and with as much detailing on the edge as possible. The paper piece should then be glued in position before applying many coats of varnish and rubbing down between coats until the raised edge of the shape is no longer visible to destroy the illusion. To give an antique look to your decoration you can add a craquelure or crackle finish, to imitate the look of old cracked varnish.

CHOOSING SCRAPS AND PIECES TO DECORATE

Start by selecting your item for decoration and then choose the paper scraps to enhance its style and shape. All sorts of wooden and tinware items are ideal for découpage. Old, worn pieces are particularly good as it is a way of renovating and decorating them at the same time. Tinware jugs, trays, cache pots, plates and boxes look lovely, particularly with the addition of a painted gold edging to finish off the design. Painted bows, stems and tiny leaves can also help a few cut-outs hang together into a good composition. Wooden trays, tables, frames, cupboards, screens and all sizes of boxes make perfect surfaces for découpage.

You can obtain your paper decorations from many different sources. Good quality wrapping paper is ideal as it is usually well printed on thin paper. Greetings cards are also good but you will need to strip off the printed surface and take most of the thick card away. To do this, stick the tip of a sharp craft knife into the edge of the card and peel off layers gradually from the back. Always work with the printed design face down on the work surface pulling back the card, rather than the print, which can tear easily.

As in the last century, it is possible to buy sheets of printed scraps which are specially made for this purpose. They usually come in partially cut out sheets, with several different sizes of the same subject, such as flowers, faces, huntsmen, Christmas motifs or cherubs. These will need to be cut out more carefully, sometimes adding more detail to the outline to enhance the shape, particularly with hair, and flower petals.

It is also tempting to use pictures from magazines but, unless the printing and paper are of the highest quality, it is unwise. The printed colours may run when varnished or the paper may go transparent and allow any print on the reverse side to show through. However, if you have found a particularly attractive design it is worth trying out a small piece of the same printing, on a spare piece of wood or tin, just in case it works well.

CUTTING OUT THE SCRAPS

To cut out découpage pieces successfully, the most important tool is a pair of small, sharp, pointed scissors that are comfortable to use. Hold the paper loosely in your left hand and cut with your right, turning the paper rather than the scissors, to follow the outline. (Reverse this if you are left-handed!) Start by cutting out lots of pieces; more than you think you will need, so

This antique footwarmer, shown with a wooden tray and table top, has a simple arrangement of flowers with a border of tiny painted gold leaves around the sides.

that you can make a really good composition, to fit the required shape. Most large floral designs look especially good when lots of flowers are arranged close together and overlapped to form

Cutting scraps

a bouquet. If the paper layers get too thick, you can trim away the underneath areas as you glue the pieces in place.

Lay the scraps out on the chosen surface and design your composition. Now is the time to choose a background colour to paint your item, so that it will enhance the découpage. Keep the scraps safely in an envelope and sketch a rough idea of your arrangement on the outside to remind you, when you start gluing.

PREPARING THE SURFACE

To prepare tinware you should rub off any old flaking paint and rust, using a wire brush. Sand any rough areas and then paint with several coats of red oxide paint, leaving it to dry thoroughly between coats. Sand this lightly with fine abrasive paper and then paint with one or two coats of matt eggshell paint. Black and dark forest green are probably the most usual colours but many smaller items look very pretty in pale blues and greens.

When the painted surface is quite dry, sand it very lightly before gluing the paper scraps in position.

To prepare wooden items, remove any old varnish and sand the surface until it is really smooth. If you want the woodgrain to remain visible under the découpage design, brush on one coat of varnish at this stage to bring out the colour of the wood. If you want a painted surface do this now, choosing either a flat colour or perhaps a dragged or sponged finish in a slightly darker colour. Brush on two or three coats of the base colour in matt emulsion or eggshell paint. Sand smooth with very fine sandpaper and then add the dragging or sponging at this stage.

GLUING THE SCRAPS

Now glue the scraps in position using PVA adhesive. This is a water-based glue which helps to protect the paper from going transparent. It is perfect for wooden surfaces but it may cause rust spots on some metal surfaces. Spread the glue thinly and evenly on to the reverse of each scrap and then press into position. Carefully trim away any excess paper if the pieces overlap several times and make the surface lumpy. Gently wipe over the glued pieces with a damp cloth to remove excess glue and smooth out any air bubbles. Leave to dry.

On metal, glue the scraps in place with clear household adhesive and wipe away any surplus immediately with a dry cloth. Paint on stems or borders at this stage using an oil-based metallic paint and a fine watercolour brush.

VARNISHING

The next stage is the varnishing. Use clear gloss varnish, either acrylic or polyurethane. You will need many layers to make a really successful finish, so be patient and allow each coat to dry properly, before putting on the next. Begin with two or three coats, leave overnight and then sand lightly with fine wet and dry sandpaper, wrapped round a sanding block. This will mostly remove the varnish over the paper cutouts so take care that you do not go through to the paper and damage it. Wipe the surface dry and remove all traces of dust, using a cloth moistened with white spirit. Repeat with two or three more coats of varnish then sand again. The number of times you repeat this process depends on the thickness of your paper decoration. Feel the surface with your fingertips to determine when it is smooth enough, but aim for about twelve coats. After the final sanding, apply just one more, very thin, coat of varnish to complete.

Spring flowers and painted gold ribbon have transformed this tiny tin trunk.

Now is the time to do the crackle finish technique if you want to give your piece an antique look. You can use a two-stage kit sold specifically for the purpose; in which case, follow the maker's instructions carefully.

You can also achieve the same effect more cheaply by buying separate ingredients. The secret of the technique is to use first an oil-based layer then a water-based layer that will react and crack evenly, without peeling off.

First apply a thin, even coat of good quality goldsize, using a bristle brush. Leave this until it is very nearly dry, just slightly sticky. Then test a small area with some of the second coating, which is gum water. Brush on a little gum water, leave for a moment and if it makes a

Old items look even more convincing with the addition of a crackle finish on the final coat of varnish to give them an antique look.

A collection of wooden and tinware items decorated in a variety of styles to complement each piece perfectly.

slight hissing sound or cracks open, leave the goldsize to dry a while longer.

When the goldsize is ready, brush on a generous coating of gum water with a soft brush and leave it to dry for about an hour. During this time the cracking will take place; you can encourage this with warm air from a hair dryer.

When the surface is dry, you can make the cracks more visible with a little artist's oil paint in raw umber or burnt sienna to imitate the dust and dirt that would have coloured an old item. Squeeze a little paint onto a saucer and dip in a cotton cloth wrapped round your fingertip. Spread the paint sparingly over the surface, rubbing it well into the cracks. Wipe off the excess with a clean cloth and leave for a few days before you give it a protective coat of the original clear varnish.

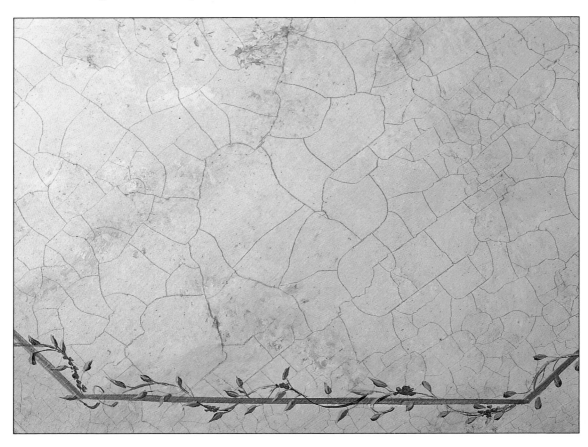

Christmas Baubles

Christmas decorations, as we know them, were virtually invented by the Victorians. The Christmas tree was the centrepiece, beautifully decorated and surrounded by gifts. These antique-look baubles are simple to make from paper balls covered with cut-out scraps from Victorian-style wrapping paper.

Cotton pulp or paper balls 5cm (2in) diameter
Small sharp scissors
Mod Podge glue/varnish
Bristle brush
Coloured cord
Victorian-style wrapping paper or découpage scraps
Sticky tape

❶ Start by cutting out lots of small scraps, similar in colour or subject matter. Try all Christmas designs, one type of flower such as pansies, or children's faces. The maximum size of the pieces should be about 5cm (2in) to cover the balls successfully. To make the paper lie flat on the curved surface of the ball, you will need to make small snips round the edge of the scrap. Try to cut along part of the design like following the petal shapes towards the centre. Test this out on the ball before you start to glue to make sure you have cut far enough.

❷ Push a ball on to an old pencil to hold it and then spread glue over about half the ball. Lay on one paper scrap and then cover this with a thin layer of glue. Put on another scrap, overlapping it slightly on the first one. Continue in this way until the ball is completely covered with no white background showing. Brush with a thin coat of glue and leave to dry, with the pencil standing up in a jam jar so that the ball does not stick to anything. Make several more balls while the first is drying and then add more layers of glue to act as a varnish.

❸ When the varnish is quite dry, remove the pencil. Cut a 10cm (4in) length of cord and tape the ends together to stop them fraying and to stiffen them. Dip the ends into the glue and push them firmly into the hole in the top of the ball. Add any small scraps round the hole to finish off the ball and then give it a final coat of Mod Podge varnish. Hang it up to dry by the cord loop.

A gorgeous Christmas tree decorated with découpage baubles and real candles in the Victorian style.

Lacework

Old Lace Pillows and Cushions

The advent of machine-made lace in the mid-nineteenth century had a widespread effect on the look of furnishings in the less well-off households. Up until that time, only the rich could afford to have the expensive handmade lace to decorate their table and bed-linen. But later, yards of the new manufactured lace could be seen adorning virtually all types of household linen, with frills, flounces and lacy edgings everywhere.

You will need to choose some old lace and embroidery from partly damaged and worn linen and combine it with modern lace, to create your cushion covers and pillow shams. Used white cotton sheeting is ideal to mount the lace on, as it is not so startlingly white as new fabric and the various shades of white from different pieces will blend better. Buy cotton lace edgings in varying widths to go with your old linen.

❶ Carefully cut away lace edgings from cloths and mats and trim off any torn parts. Join the pieces carefully, by hand, using French seams to hide the raw edges. Use this to make edgings and frills.

Stitching lace together to form a square

❷ Use corner areas and centre pieces from tablecloths to make the central part of your cushion cover. Cut out the motifs, leaving a margin of fabric all round and then join them into a square with machine-stitched flat seams. Using pinking shears, trim away any raw seam edges that show through close to the stitching. Press the seams open.

❸ Lay the joined lace centrally on to a piece of sheeting 8cm (3in) larger all round than your cushion pad and tack (baste) in place. Tack (baste) old or modern lace edgings round the sides (mitring the corners) to cover any raw edges and then machine stitch. Insert ribbons in slotted lace and add bows as you wish.

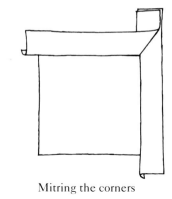

Mitring the corners

❹ Appliqué old lace mats on to sheeting. Tack (baste) in place first, across the middle and round the edge and then zigzag machine stitch round some central motifs and lastly all round the edge, to hold in place.

❺ To make the pattern piece for the cushion back, draw out a square to the same size as the front. Fold the square in half and, adding 1.5cm (⅝in) to one side of the square, cut out two pieces of backing fabric. Machine stitch taking a 1.5cm (⅝in) seam and leaving a gap for inserting the pad. Place the cushion pieces with right

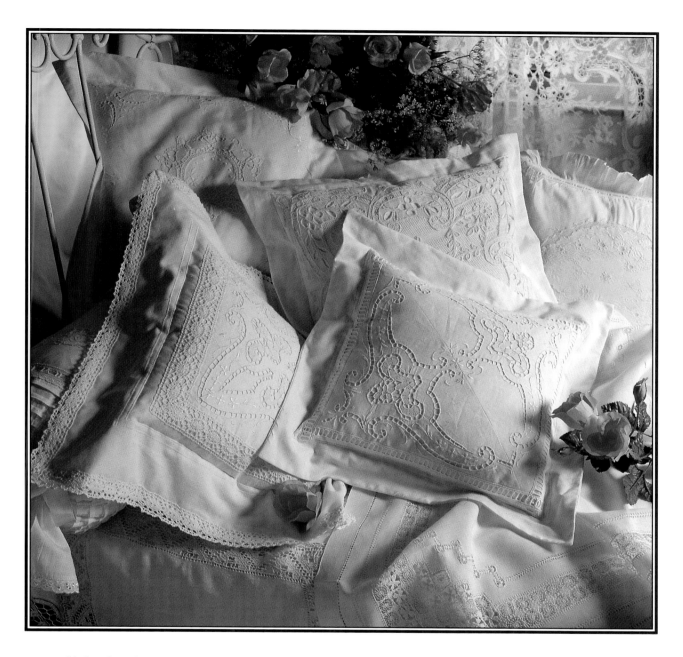

Make a luxurious heap of white lace cushions in all shapes and sizes to dress up your bedroom.

---

sides together and stitch all round 1.5cm (⅝in) from the edge.

❻ Turn right sides out and press. Mark a line 5cm (2in) away from the edge and work a line of machine satin stitch over it, through both layers of fabric. This will form the decorative border around the cushion, which you can edge with lace if you wish. Lastly, insert the cushion pad and add ribbon ties or hand stitch the opening to neaten.

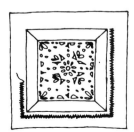

Stitching cushion border

Tape Lace

As the name suggests, this type of lacework is made using special tape. It is loosely woven with a gathering thread down the edge so that you can pull it into various shapes to follow a pattern and then anchor it in place with decorative stitching. Once you have mastered the technique with a small item like a mat or dressing table set, you can go on to make beautiful table-cloths and bedspreads. This type of lace originated in the seventeenth century and was copied extensively in the Victorian era in many countries; missionaries even took patterns to the Far East. Tape lace has many different names and variations and so its sources are rather difficult to trace.

MAT

8mm (5/16 in) wide white lace tape with a plain edge
White DMC coton à broder special 25
Pins
Tracing paper
A black waterproof felt-tipped pen
Stiff muslin
Tapestry and sewing needles

---

❶ Trace off the pattern from the following page on to the tracing paper, using the felt-tipped pen. Lay this over the stiff muslin and tack or tape round the edge to hold the layers in place. Find the gathering thread in one edge of the lace tape and pull this gently to coil the tape. It should lie flat on itself but if it is distorted, cut off this piece and find the correct thread. You will soon get used to doing this correctly. Gently gather up about 1m (1yd) of the tape.

❷ Beginning at the point on the pattern (overleaf) marked with an arrow, start shaping and then pinning the tape in position, following the parallel lines. Pin through all three layers of tape, tracing paper and muslin. When the tape is pinned in place all the way round, cut the tape, leaving about 1.5cm (5/8in) extra and fold

under the raw ends neatly. Next, pin the inner circle and then the central curved diamond. For the diamond shape you will need to fold the tape at the corners so that the gathering edge stays on the outside edge of the diamond. Start and finish at a corner.

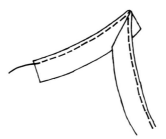

Folding corners on diamond shape

❸ Tack (baste) the tapes to the pattern through all the layers using a contrasting thread so that you can remove it easily later. Follow the outside edges of curves as they tend to stand away from the pattern more than the inner edges. Make small regular stitches to anchor the tape accurately. Remove the pins.

Begin by making this simple lace mat then graduate to the beautiful bedspread, featuring tape lace with whitework embroidery.

❹ Using fine white thread, the same thickness as the thread used to make the tape, lightly stitch the tape layers together where they overlap or cross and at the joins. These stitches should be even and as invisible as possible on the right side. Do not start sewing with a knot, but make two or three tiny backstitches to anchor the thread securely. Do not pull the stitches tightly or the work will not lie flat.

❺ Next is the embroidery stage, where the spaces are filled with various stitches and areas of tape are joined, to hold the whole shape together. Using the coton à broder and a round-ended tapestry needle, start with the insertion or Russian stitch, in the scallops on the edge of

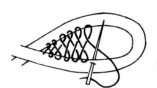

Insertion stitch

the mat. Anchor the thread as before and take a small stitch in one edge of the tape, take another stitch in the opposite edge from right to left and then come back to the first edge. Keep stitches even, without pulling the tapes out of shape, making about four complete stitches in each scallop. On every other scallop, make two vertical lines of thread. Take the first thread over and under the herringbone stitches and anchor it at the end then work back up the same thread going under and over the opposite way and also round the first thread to give a twisted effect.

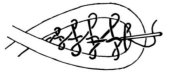

Working the central vein

❻ Next join the circle to the scallops with a knotted insertion stitch. Work as follows from right to left; bring the thread up on the lower edge, go across to the upper edge and take a

small stitch. Put the needle behind the first stitch and over and under the loose thread. Pull gently to form the knot and take a stitch in the lower edge. Continue in this way all round the circle.

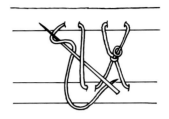

Knotted insertion stitch

❼ Then join the diamond to the circle with a simple lacing stitch that is gathered into three strands with a central thread. Work back and forth across the space to make about 15 fairly loose, vertical stitches. When you reach the end of each area, turn the work round and make a bar across the centre. Go down over the first three vertical threads to the back of the work. Then up, behind the threads to gather them together. Put the needle the other side of the horizontal thread and back under the three threads. Repeat this until you reach the end and then start on the next area.

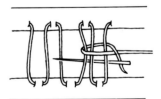

Gathered lacing stitch

❽ Lastly fill the space in the centre of the diamond with spider web stitches. Start in one corner and run a thread across to the opposite corner. Go down one side making two more threads parallel to the first one. This should bring you out at the third corner. Repeat the process, going across to the opposite corner and then back and forth. Keep doing this until you have ten threads crossing each other in the central area. Where four threads cross, make a spider web by working round this point going under and over each thread three or four times.

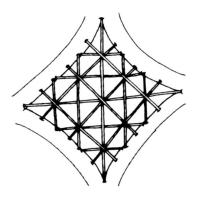

Spider web mesh

⑩ If you wish to use this design as the centre of a larger mat or table-cloth, lay it on top of fine cotton fabric and tack it carefully in place. Using a small, close-set, machine zigzag stitch, sew all round the outer edge making sure you catch the edge of the tape securely. Turn over the work and very carefully snip away the fabric from behind the lace taking care not to cut any of the stitching threads.

⑨ When you have finished the embroidery, take out the contrasting tacking (basting) threads and check to see that everything is joined properly. Press the lace firmly under a damp cloth using a hot iron, to flatten and secure the shape. Just press and lift the iron without moving it back and forth, which may distort the lace.

Working spider
web stitch

Begin here

Pattern for tape lace mat

Shellwork

Shellwork

The Victorians loved the seaside and the collecting of seaweed, shells and pebbles became quite an obsession with many ladies. Large shells were collected as specimens, while smaller shells in a variety of shapes and colours were used to decorate boxes, frames, mirrors and a myriad of small souvenirs. (For key to shells, see overleaf.)

One secret of making successful shell projects is to choose the shells carefully to fit the space available. It is worth spending some time sorting shells into sizes before you begin gluing them in position. Even a handful of the same type of shell can vary considerably in size or colour, and if the patterns and shapes are to remain uniform it is quite important to use exactly the same shells all over each area. Use modern PVA and clear household adhesives which dry clear and almost invisible. Instead of spreading the whole area with the adhesive it is much better to dab a little glue on to the base of each shell and then press it into place. Put some glue on to the adjoining shells as well, so that the whole arrangement is really secure.

If you are using any other materials with the shells, like pictures, fabric or braid, attach these to the surface first then glue the shells in place slightly overlapping the edges. When making pictures, work with the backing board in position in the frame, so that you can place the shells right up to the frame without leaving a gap.

A modern octagonal sailors' valentine picture using about ten different kinds of tiny shells to create the intricate patterns.

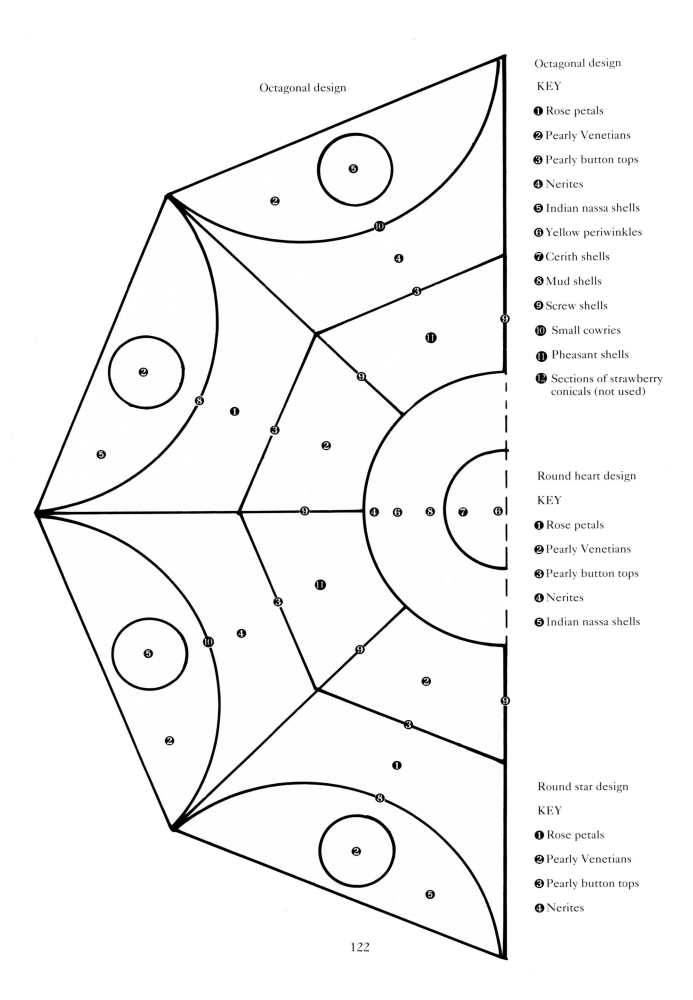

Octagonal design

Octagonal design

KEY

❶ Rose petals

❷ Pearly Venetians

❸ Pearly button tops

❹ Nerites

❺ Indian nassa shells

❻ Yellow periwinkles

❼ Cerith shells

❽ Mud shells

❾ Screw shells

❿ Small cowries

⓫ Pheasant shells

⓬ Sections of strawberry conicals (not used)

Round heart design

KEY

❶ Rose petals

❷ Pearly Venetians

❸ Pearly button tops

❹ Nerites

❺ Indian nassa shells

Round star design

KEY

❶ Rose petals

❷ Pearly Venetians

❸ Pearly button tops

❹ Nerites

122

Round heart design

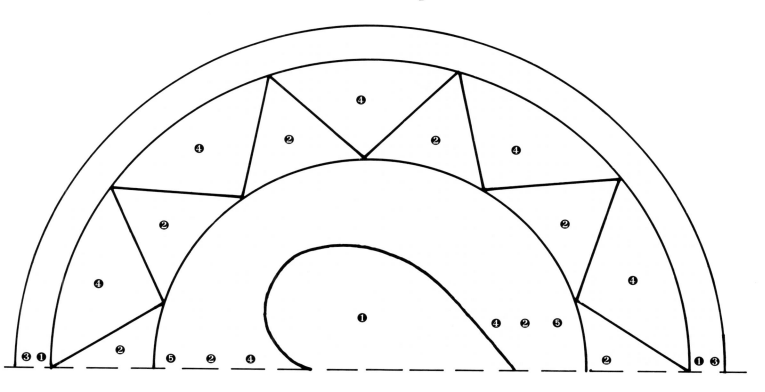

Round star design

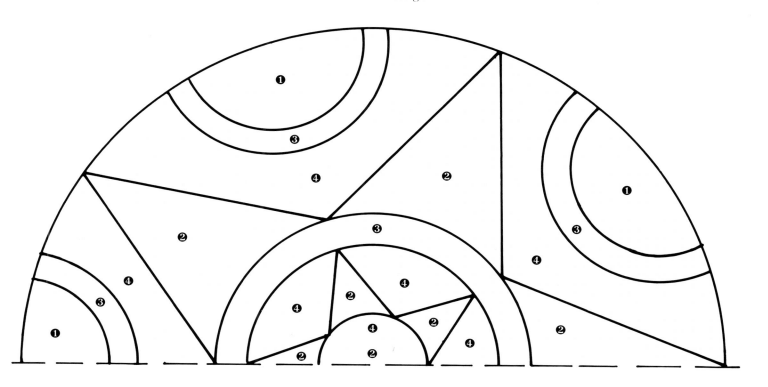

Sailors' Valentines

Sailors' valentines were popular throughout the nineteenth century and were thought to have been made by sailors on long voyages to bring home to their loved ones. Such pictures often depicted a heart shape or motto, worked in the centre of an intricate mosaic of many sorts of small shells. Here are designs and instructions to make your own modern sailors' valentine. There are two round designs and one octagonal (see page 121), though you could use different frames and shells, with the following instructions as a guide.

An assortment of at least 10 different types of shells
PVA glue and spreader
Thick white card for the backing
3 picture frames - 2 circular wooden frames
*   24cm (9.5in) diameter and an octagonal frame*
*   36cm (14in) across*
Tweezers

---

❶ All three pictures are made in the same way. First cut out a piece of the thick card to fit into the frame rebate. Place it in the frame and draw round the inner edge, to outline the area to be covered with shells.

❷ Trace out the designs (pages 122/3) and draw them out on to the card in pencil. Arrange the shells on the design, following the patterns. It is best to start at the centre of the design and work outwards. Try out the shells in each area before you glue them in place. Then glue the shells round the outline of each area first, and fill in the centre, packing the shells as close together as possible to cover the card. This method helps to keep the pattern lines accurate.

❸ In each area of the design, use only shells of the same colour, tone and type and keep them facing the same way. Alternate areas of light and dark shells to define the pattern. Put the shell covered card into the frame before you reach the outer edge, then glue the last shells on to the card in situ, to make sure they fit snugly inside the frame.

Here I describe each design as it was made, but you may have different frames and other types of shells so only use this as a guide.

OCTAGONAL DESIGN

Begin at the centre with a single yellow periwinkle, then encircle it with brown striped cerith shells. Work outwards with circles of mud shells, yellow periwinkles, and nerites.

Next divide the surrounding area equally with eight screw shells and fill in the shapes between them alternately with pearly Venetians and pheasant shells.

Now glue on an octagonal outline and radiating lines of pearly button tops. Form the semi-circles around the outer edge alternately with mud shells and small cowries. Fill in every alternate semi-circle with pearly Venetians and a circle of tiny pale Indian nassa shells. Fill remaining semi-circles with Indian nassa shells and circles of pearly Venetians. Cover remaining areas alternately with rose petals and nerites.

ROUND HEART DESIGN

Begin by gluing on the central heart shape in small rose petal shells, then surround it with

Choose a heart or star design to make your own unusual valentine.

several rows of shells such as pearly Venetians, nerites and Indian nassa shells until you reach the inner circle.

Fill in the points of the star with pearly Venetians then, between the two outer circles, make a border of pearly button tops with a tiny rose petal shell tucked between each one. Fill in the remaining areas with nerites, adding one pearly button top at the centre of the outer edge.

ROUND STAR DESIGN

Begin at the centre with a large nerite, encircled first with a ring of pearly Venetians, then with a ring of tiny nerites. Fill in the points of the large and small stars with pearly Venetians and fill the ring between them with circles of pearly button tops, rose petals, Indian nassa shells and similar types. Outline the semi-circles with pearly button tops and fill them in with rose petal shells. Cover the remaining areas with nerites and one pink-coloured mud shell at the top of each semi-circle.

Shell Boxes, Frames and Mirror

These projects are typical of Victorian souvenirs. The little round box is modern with the top left as bare wood and the base painted pink then rubbed over with a rough gold top-coat. I have lined the oblong box with some old blue silk ribbon and tiny beads. The outside has a dull gold finish, ideal for the pearly shells. The little frames are very inexpensive, unfinished wood and their covering of shells is a quick and easy way of making them into lovely gifts. The mirror would be an ideal project for displaying a few larger shells.

RECTANGULAR BOX

A small rectangular wooden box
A selection of pearly Venetians, pearly button tops,
  grey nerites and button top shells
Sandpaper
PVA glue
Mod Podge glue/varnish
Gold bronzing powder
FOR THE BOX LINING
Thin card
Scraps of silk
Scraps of thin wadding
Tiny coloured beads
Fine needle and thread

❶ Sandpaper the box until the surface is smooth and free from varnish. Mix up some of the bronzing powder with Mod Podge and use this to paint the box all over, inside and out. When the box is dry, try out an arrangement of shells to cover the top of the box, alternating rows of light and dark shells. Keep the shells facing the same way in each row, to look uniform. When you are happy with the design, glue them in place with the PVA glue.

❷ To line the box, cut out rectangles of card to fit easily inside the top, base and sides of the box. Cut out a piece of wadding the same size as each card shape, and a piece of silk a little larger. Lightly glue the wadding to the card, lay the silk on the work surface and place the card on top, centrally, with the wadding downwards. Bring the fabric round the edges of the card and glue to the back neatly. Mark even, criss-cross lines on the back of each piece of card and use this as a guide to stitch on tiny beads to slightly quilt the surface of the silk. Glue the base piece in place inside the box first and then the side pieces to complete.

ROUND BOX

A small round wooden box
A small selection of rose petal shells and pearly
  Venetians
Sandpaper
Greetings card
Mod Podge glue/varnish
PVA glue ·
Pink gloss paint for the base of the box
Gold bronzing powder
Small brushes

❶ First sandpaper the surface of the box lid to make it smooth and free from varnish. Cut out a

Re-create the mood of the seaside with a group of shell-encrusted frames, a box and any seaside mementoes from the past or present.

126

Small wooden picture frames
A selection of small shells as for the boxes
PVA glue

Make the frames in the same way as the rectangular box. You can leave the frames as bare wood or paint them in gold. Use a selection of small shells to completely cover the front of the frames. Start by gluing on the row of shells on the inside edge of the frame, then arrange the corners and lastly the outside edge. Choose rows of shells that contrast well in shape and colour and glue them on facing the same direction in each row.

MIRROR

A pine-framed mirror about 31 × 27cm (12 × 10½in)
  with flat moulding about 4cm (1½in) wide
4 scallop shells for the corners of the frame
A good selection of decorative, medium-sized shells
About 100 pearly button top shells
PVA glue

If possible, work with the mirror out of the frame, to avoid marking it with glue. Working on a flat surface, experiment with your selection of shells to decorate the frame. A row of pearly button tops next to the mirror is a good starting point, but lay the corner scallop shells in place before gluing, to make sure you leave enough room for them.

Glue the shells in groups at the corners and at the centre of each side of the frame. Add a few more smaller shells to link these groups and to finish the frame. Keep the design regular and match up the shells on each side of the frame for a balanced look.

Replace the mirror into the frame and seal in place with card and gummed paper tape to protect it.

This modern pine-framed mirror has been given the Victorian look with a carefully chosen selection of shells, some bought and some collected.

small scrap from a greetings card or wrapping paper, to decorate the centre of the box lid. For a curved top like this one, you will need to cut in towards the centre of the paper scrap, to help it lie flat on the surface of the lid. Glue it in place and then paint two coats of Mod Podge over the paper scrap to seal it. Leave to dry.

❷ Paint the base of the box in pink, or a colour that will go well with the picture on the lid. Leave to dry thoroughly. Mix up a little gold bronzing powder with some Mod Podge and brush this roughly over the paint so that some of the colour shows through. Leave to dry again and then coat with one more layer of Mod Podge to seal.

❸ Using the PVA glue, stick on a row of medium-sized, rose petal shells along the edge of the lid. Next glue on a row of small pearly Venetians and lastly a row of tiny rose petal shells. Push the shells really close together, interlocking the shapes, to make a pretty edge to the picture.

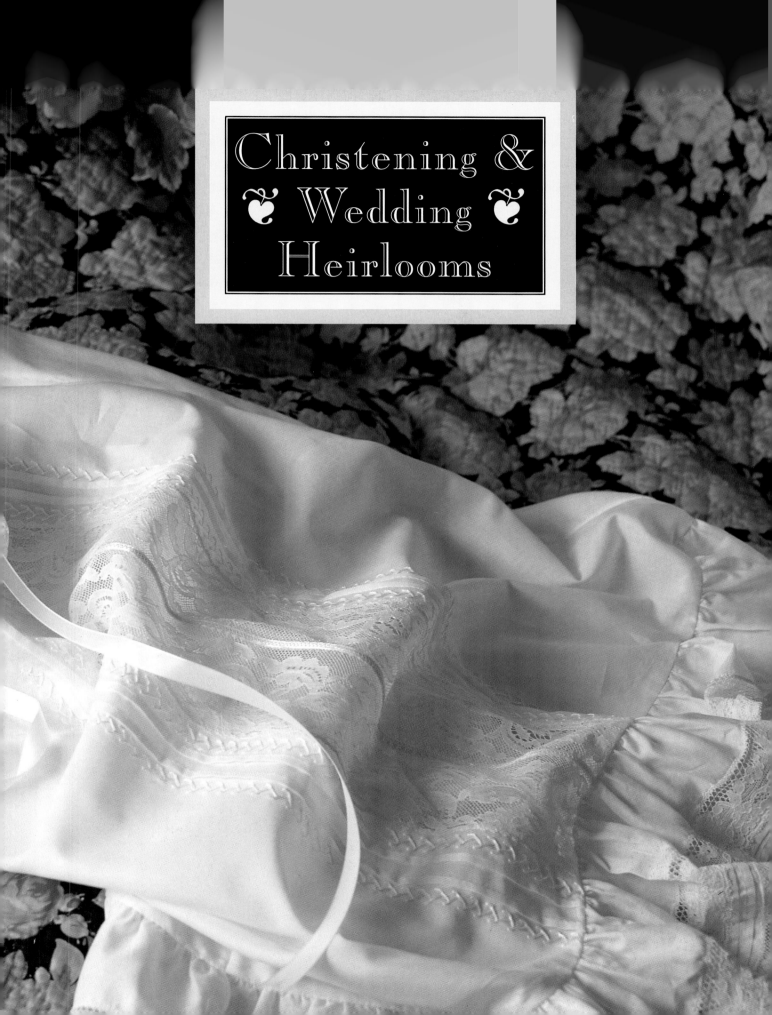

Christening & ❦ Wedding ❦ Heirlooms

Christening Robe

This christening robe is a simple pattern that has been given the traditional look with frills, pin-tucking, ribbon and lace appliqué, and hand embroidery. It is quite a labour of love and will last through many generations like the original Victorian heirlooms.

3m (3¼yd) of fine white lawn 115cm (45in) wide
Fine white cotton lace as follows:
  1.50m (1⅝yd) lace × 7cm (2¾in) wide
  3m (3¼yd) lace × 3.5cm (1¼in) wide
  4.20m (4½yd) × 13mm (½in) wide
50cm (⅝yd) narrow edging lace
1.60m (1¾yd) narrow, white picot-edged satin ribbon
1.60m (1¾yd) narrow, white satin ribbon
3 skeins of white DMC stranded embroidery cotton (floss)
White sewing thread
50cm (18in) narrow elastic
Soluble embroidery marker pen
Thin tracing paper
Graph paper

Note: Work 13mm (½in) seams throughout unless indicated, oversew seam edges or use french seams to neaten. Each square on the pattern (overleaf) equals 2cm (¾in).

❶ Using graph paper, draw out the christening robe pattern to full size. Copy each line, square by square, for an accurate shape. Trace and cut out the pieces in thin tracing paper. Mark on all the details as shown.

❷ Begin by working the pin-tucking, appliqué and embroidery for the bodice and sleeves before you cut out the pattern pieces. Starting with the bodice, cut out a piece of fabric 46 × 18cm (18 × 7in). Fold in half across the width and press the fold. Using the bodice pleating diagram, measure and mark the lines using a ruler and soluble embroidery marker pen. Bring the lines together so that the folds are on the right side of the fabric. Tack (baste) and stitch these pin-tucks in place. Press the pin-tucks flat, working away from the centre fold. Now stitch on the ribbon and lace as shown in the photograph, using straight stitch for the ribbon and a tiny zigzag stitch along both edges of the lace.

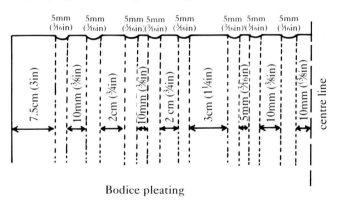

Bodice pleating

❸ Turn the piece of fabric over and very carefully cut away the fabric from behind the rows of lace. Use small sharp embroidery scissors and take care not to cut the stitches or the lace. Lastly embroider lines of chain-stitch and feather stitch, as indicated, using three strands of embroidery cotton.

Chain-stitch

Feather stitch

❹ Cut out two pieces of fabric 23 × 33cm (9 × 13in) for the sleeves. Fold in half across the width and press. Follow the diagram carefully and sew the pin-tucks, ribbon and lace, as for the bodice.

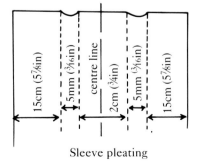

Sleeve pleating

❺ Pin the bodice and sleeve pattern pieces to the decorated fabric and cut out as directed.

Line up the centre fold with the marked centre line on each piece. Now pin in place and cut out all the other pattern pieces, as directed, also cutting a 14cm (5½in) × 3m (3¼yd) frill piece all along one selvedge.

❻ On the skirt front, stitch on the two strips of lace, overlapping the centre line slightly. Stitch on the ribbon with zigzag stitch, to cover the centre line and then trim away the fabric from behind. Stitch two pin-tucks either side of the lace and then work the four lines of feather stitch, in white, as indicated.

❼ With right sides together, pin and tack (baste) the shoulder and side seams to join the back and front bodice pieces. Stitch in place.

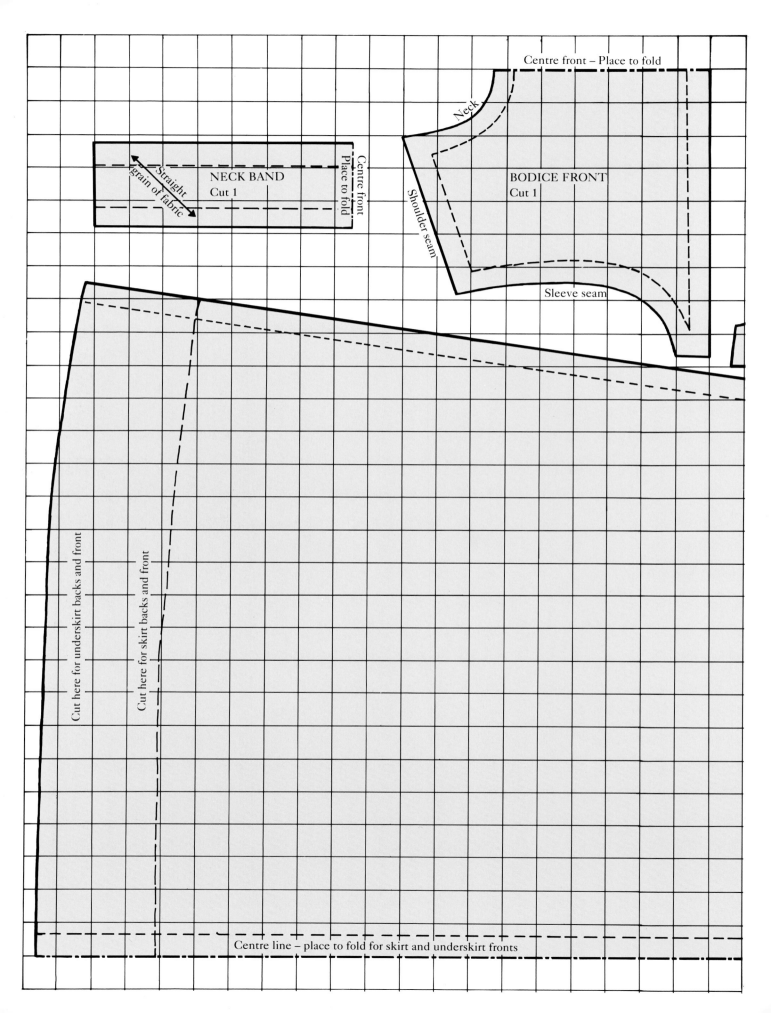

NECK BAND
Cut 1

Straight
grain of fabric

Centre front
Place to fold

Centre front – Place to fold

Neck

BODICE FRONT
Cut 1

Shoulder seam

Sleeve seam

Cut here for underskirt backs and front

Cut here for skirt backs and front

Centre line – place to fold for skirt and underskirt fronts

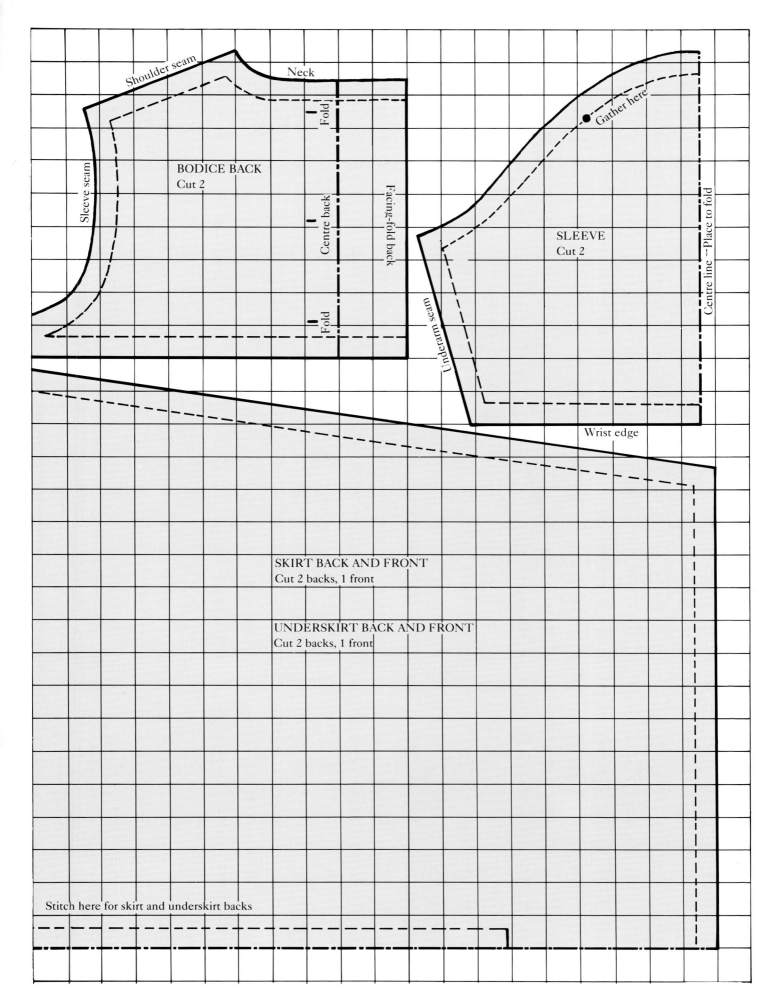

❽ Cut two 4cm (1½in) wide strips of fabric along the selvedge, to go along the wrist edge of each sleeve. Stitch some of the narrow edging lace along each selvedge. Now line up the other edge with the wrist edge of the sleeves, with right sides together. Pin, tack (baste) and stitch. Press this seam down towards the lace edging and make another row of stitching, through all the layers, to form a narrow channel for the elastic. Embroider a row of feather stitch just below the channel. Using a bodkin, thread some of the narrow elastic into each channel. Do not gather the elastic but leave the ends free. Pin and tack (baste) the underarm seams with right sides together. Stitch this seam, pulling up the elastic as you reach it, so that the wrist measures about 14cm (5½in) round, when gathered. Stitch through the elastic to hold it in place then trim off the ends.

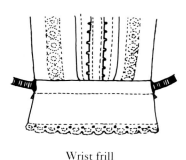

Wrist frill

❾ Run two rows of gathering stitches, between the dots and either side of the seam line, on the top of each sleeve. Insert the sleeve into the bodice, matching up the raw edges and with right sides together. Line up the dots and the underarm seams. Pull up the gathering threads so that the head of the sleeve fits the top of the armhole. Pin, tack (baste) and stitch the sleeves in place. Remove the gathering and tacking (basting) threads. Press under the facings at the centre back of the bodice and stitch.

❿ With right sides together, and raw edges matching, pin, tack (baste) and stitch the neckband round the neck of the bodice. Fold this over to the inside, turn the raw edges under and slipstitch to neaten. Stitch a piece of the edging lace to the folded edge of the neckband. Embroider a row of chain-stitch and a row of feather stitch all round to decorate.

⓫ Pin, tack (baste) and stitch the skirt front to the skirt back pieces at the side seams. Cut and join the skirt frill pieces to make a strip about 3m (3¼yd) long with the selvedge running along one long edge. Stitch some of the 13mm (½in) wide lace to the selvedge of the frill. Make two pin tucks above this and then stitch on the medium-width lace just above. Trim away the fabric from behind the lace. Gather along the raw edge of the frill and pull up the threads evenly, to fit round the bottom of the skirt. With right sides together and raw edges matching, pin and tack (baste) the frill to the skirt. Stitch and then remove the tacking (basting) and gathering threads.

⓬ With right sides together, pin, tack (baste) and stitch the centre back seam on the skirt as far as the dot. Fold under the remaining seam allowance on each side for the opening and stitch to neaten. Gather along the top edge of the skirt and pull up the threads to fit round the lower edge of the bodice. With right sides together and raw edges matching, pin and tack (baste) the skirt to the bodice.

⓭ Make up the underskirt in the same way but just stitch one piece of the narrow lace to the lower edge instead of the frill. Tack (baste) the gathered underskirt in place to the lower edge of the bodice and then stitch all the layers together. Remove the gathering threads and neaten the seam. Stitch lengths of plain satin ribbon to the centre back of the robe as marked and tie to close. Make a bow from the remaining satin ribbon and stitch it to the front of the robe at the waist.

Close-up view of the detailed work on the bodice and sleeves to guide your embroidery and appliqué.

Pot-pourri Balls

The Victorians were great lovers of sweet-smelling herbs to scent their clothes and linens and they made all sorts of ingenious and pretty sachets in which to display them. These decorative lacy balls can be filled with dried lavender or pot-pourri to make pretty hangings for the wardrobe or anywhere in the bedroom. They would make lovely bridesmaids' gifts, or a collection for the bride herself.

Circles of fine white cotton lawn
White cotton lace for edgings and frills in varying
*   widths*
White satin ribbon, picot-edged and plain
Scraps of polyester wadding
Matching sewing thread
Pot-pourri and dried lavender

LARGE BALL

❶ Cut out a circle of fabric 46cm (18in) diameter. Using a small zigzag stitch, sew a piece of 6.5cm (2½in) wide cotton lace all round the edge. Where the ends of the lace meet, overlap them and turn in the raw edges. Hand stitch to neaten.

❷ Using doubled sewing thread, make a line of gathering stitches 9cm (3½in) from the lace edging. Pull up the gathers slightly to make a bag and push in some wadding. Put some pot-pourri or lavender on top and then fill up the space with more wadding to make a ball. Pull up the gathers tightly to close the bag completely and then tie the ends together securely. Roll it in your hands to make a good round shape.

❸ To make a frill, cut a strip of fabric 38 × 5cm (15 × 2in). Stitch wide lace to one long edge and narrow lace to the other long edge. Run a line of gathering stitches along the middle of the fabric. Pull up the gathers and place the frill

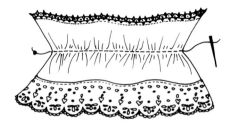

Making a frill for the large pot-pourri ball

round the neck of the ball, with the wider lace at the bottom. Tie the threads securely and hand stitch the raw ends of the frill together. Finish off the ball with a loop and a bow, in picot-edged satin ribbon.

MEDIUM SIZED BALL

Cut a circle of fabric 23cm (9in) diameter. Stitch 7.5cm (3in) wide lace all round the edge. Run the gathering just below the lace and gather and fill the ball as before, omitting the frill. Decorate with a double bow of plain and picot-edged satin ribbon.

SMALL BALL

Cut out a circle of fabric 15cm (6in) in diameter. Stitch 5cm (2in) wide lace all round the edge. Gather just below the lace and fill as before omitting the frill. Finish with a loop of plain ribbon stitched inside the top of the ball and a bow stitched to the front.

Whitework Pillowslip and Mat

Whitework embroidery was a favourite way of decorating plain linen and underclothes in Victorian times. It consisted of intricate white embroidery on white linen so the effect was subtle and textured rather than colourful. Probably the most delicate work came from Scotland and was copied in England and Ireland by virtually every needle-woman. The designs varied from simple initials to impressive monograms and all sorts of patterns both classical and natural.

PILLOWSLIP

The pillowslip I have embroidered is for a baby's cot but you can adapt this corner motif to fit any sized pillowslip, to make a set for yourself or as a superb wedding present.

A ready-made pillowslip
Soluble embroidery marker pen or dressmaker's
  carbon paper.
Thin tracing paper
Fine black waterproof felt-tipped pen
White DMC stranded embroidery cotton (floss)
  (about two skeins for each complete motif)
Fine crewel needle

Trace off the full-sized motif. Draw it in a fine black line and trim the tracing paper so that it will fit inside the pillowslip with the motif in one corner, near the edge. Lay it on a smooth work surface and draw the design through with the embroidery marker. Alternatively you can pin the paper pattern and carbon paper to the outside of the pillowslip and then transfer the design by following the lines with a ballpoint pen. Divide the embroidery cotton (floss) into three strands and begin by following all the double outlines with chain-stitch (see page 132). When you have completed this, embroider the single lines with stem stitch and the short dotted lines with a single straight stitch. Complete the design with the circles embroi-

dered in satin stitch and the dots as french knots. For the word Baby, work in satin stitch and a double row of stem stitch.

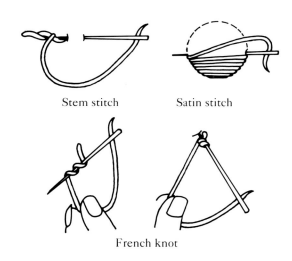

Stem stitch   Satin stitch

French knot

Using a sponge dipped in clean water dab the embroidered area to remove all traces of the embroidery marker pen. Press on the reverse.

DRESSING TABLE MAT

This pretty mat is perfect for a dressing table or you could use it on a tray or for a placemat. It is a simple naturalistic design with flowers and

Embroidered in whitework this baby pillowslip would make the perfect christening keepsake.

¼ pattern for mat

Buttonhole stitch

foliage all embroidered in chain-stitch with a traditional border of buttonhole stitch to neaten the scalloped edge.

White cotton lawn 40cm (16in) square
A large embroidery hoop
Tracing and transfer materials as for the pillowslip
A fine crewel needle
White DMC coton à broder special 25
Sharp scissors

Trace off the quarter circle design as for the pillowslip and transfer it to the fabric to form a circle. Mount the fabric in the embroidery hoop. Using one strand of the embroidery cotton, follow all the lines with a tiny chain-stitch. (See pillowslip.)

Work the scalloped outline in buttonhole stitch and very carefully snip away the excess fabric outside the buttonhole stitching. Try to cut as near as possible to the embroidery without cutting the threads. Press on the reverse side.

Index

Page numbers in italics indicate illustrations